HMS ALBION
1944 – 1973
The Old Grey Ghost

Neil McCart

FOREWORD BY ADMIRAL OF THE FLEET
SIR WILLIAM STAVELEY GCB DL

To all ex-*Albions* 1954-1973

Front Cover. A magnificent water-colour painting by New Zealand artist Brian Conroy showing *Albion* in antipodean waters during her 1958/59 world cruise.

Inside Front Cover. Full power trials 1954. *(B. Lyons)*

Inside Back Cover. Full power trials 1969. *(M. Ollivant)*

Cover Design by Caroline McCart

© Neil McCart/FAN PUBLICATIONS 1995
ISBN: 0 9519538 6 9

Typesetting By: Highlight Type Bureau Ltd,
2 Clifton Villas, Bradford, West Yorkshire BD8 7BY

Printing By: The Amadeus Press Ltd,
517 Leeds Road, Huddersfield,
West Yorkshire HD2 1YJ

Published By FAN PUBLICATIONS
17 Wymans Lane, Cheltenham, GL51 9QA, England. Fax & Tel 01242 580290

Contents

Foreword

During the east of Suez leg of *Albion's* last commission it was my good fortune to work with her as Captain of a different type of amphibious ship, *Intrepid*. We both had active roles in the final withdrawals from the British bases in the Far East and the Gulf. My surprise was only equalled by my pleasure to be told that I was to succeed Rear-Admiral Jungius in early June 1972.

I first saw her at sea looking as smart as can be before the Queen's review of the Home Fleet in the Cromarty Firth in 1957. Whilst in *Cavalier* in 1958 we operated with her off Sumatra. After her conversion to a commando carrier we of The Inshore Flotilla worked with her off Borneo. From these encounters I knew she had a great tradition as a 'Can Do' well run and very happy ship. Being in her company was always stimulating and she had a deservedly good reputation for providing fresh bread and other help to the smaller ships around her.

The span of her active life encompassed the translation from British Empire into Commonwealth. The balance between the Cold War requirements within the NATO area and the historical Empire commitments in the Middle and Far East was such that until the withdrawal from east of Suez in 1971/72 much of her time was spent in those areas playing an active part in the various crises of those times.

During 1972 hope sprang eternal about her future as an LPH until Lord Carrington had the courtesy to visit the ship personally as Secretary of State for Defence during 'Exercise Strong Express' in the Norwegian Fjords to tell me that a final decision had been taken that the ship was to be paid off and either sold or scrapped. Having to tell the ship's company was my saddest moment.

In this book Neil McCart describes so well the record of a great ship manned by great people who made her happy and efficient. In doing so they upheld the fine traditions of the Royal Navy and the Royal Marines serving our country well.

William Staveley
Admiral of the Fleet
March 1995

Chapter One

An Inauspicious Start

On 23 March 1944 the British Press told of the Red Army's increased bridgehead on the right bank of the River Dniester as they stood ready to enter Hungary and Romania. The Soviet army had broken Hitler's much vaunted *Wehrmacht* and in Italy, despite setbacks at Monte Cassino, US and Commonwealth troops were advancing north. Although it was not reflected in the media reports, in southern England preparations for the amphibious landings on the northern coast of France were nearing their completion. Also taking place on 23 March, amid these momentous events, was a small ceremony at the Wallsend-on-Tyne shipyard of Swan Hunter & Wigham Richardson to mark the laying of the first keel plates of the light fleet aircraft-carrier HMS *Albion*.

By 1943 the aircraft-carrier was considered by many to be the new status symbol of maritime power. The immense striking capacity of its aircraft gave it an effectiveness which was far greater than any previous type of capital ship. This power had been first demonstrated by the Royal Navy in November 1940, when 24 torpedo-carrying Swordfish from HMS *Illustrious* attacked the Italian fleet at Taranto. In the appropriately named 'Operation Judgement' the Royal Navy had, at one stroke, immobilized almost half of the Italian Fleet.

HMS *Albion* was ordered in 1943 when, although an Allied victory was assured in the long term, the end of the war was by no means in sight. Originally it had been intended that there would be eight new ships of the Centaur class, which would be named *Albion*, *Centaur* (keel laid 30 May 1944), *Elephant* (keel laid 21 June 1944), *Bulwark* (keel laid 10 May 1945), *Hermes*, *Arrogant*, *Monmouth* and *Polyphemus*. In the event the latter four never left the drawing-board as their contracts were cancelled in October 1945,

and the *Elephant* was renamed *Hermes*. Following the sudden end to the war against Japan the government's priorities changed and most of the country's shipbuilding capacity was given over to the merchant fleet. This fact, together with the shortages of skilled labour and steel, meant that progress on the *Albion* (and her sister ships) was slow and it was the spring of 1947 before the hull was ready for launching.

In those austere days, following the end of the Second World War, the ceremony itself was rather a low-key affair which was not helped by the vagaries of the British weather. However, despite high winds and pouring rain on Tuesday 6 May 1947, crowds lined both banks of the River Tyne to see Mrs Violet Attlee, the wife of the Prime Minister, pull the launching levers and send the *Albion* stern first into the water. Even as Mrs Attlee and the other VIPs present left the launch platform for the official luncheon, the tugs were towing the carrier's hull to a lay-up berth in the river where she was secured to buoys and left in the care of a small maintenance party for over two years. In May 1947 Britain's crippling war debts stood at over

A poor quality, but rare, montage with shots taken on the day that *Albion* was launched. *Top*: The crowd brave the wind and rain to watch the launch at the Swan Hunter shipyard. *Centre*: The *Albion* in the waters of the River Tyne for the first time and *Circled*: Mrs Violet Attlee pulls the launching lever.

The *Albion* laid up on the Tyne on 15 May 1947, nine days after her launch. She would remain at this berth for over two years.

£300 million and in the shops even the utility products were rationed. Despite the country's world-wide commitments, the government's priority was the very necessary export drive and the urgent building of merchant shipping and so the *Albion* lay at her berth in the river, presenting a somewhat forlorn and neglected picture. However, the new aircraft-carrier had not been forgotten by the Admiralty, and on 21 June 1947 the Deputy Contoller of the Navy, Admiral Sir Alexander Madden CBE, formally approved the ship's badge which is described in the heraldic records as a 'lion sejant', a sitting lion. The name itself, *Albion*, was the ancient Roman and Greek name for the island of Britain, derived from the Latin 'albus', meaning 'white', on account of the chalk cliffs along the coast around Dover. The name 'Albion' is still a poetic term for Great Britain, the Gaelic form being 'Alban' or 'Albany'.

Finally in August 1949 it was announced that work would be resumed on the *Albion* and that the new aircraft-carrier would be completed and commissioned in the summer of 1953. (Work was also resumed on the *Bulwark* and *Centaur* which had been laid up at Belfast). However, as she had been lying idle in the River Tyne the underwater hull would obviously require maintenance and it was decided

that this would be carried out at Rosyth, where she could be dry docked, before being returned to Swan Hunter's shipyard at Wallsend for the construction work and fitting out to be completed.

At this time, although her main propulsion machinery had been fitted, the *Albion* was literally just an empty shell. She had no island superstructure and there were gaping holes in the flight deck where, eventually, her hangar lifts would be fitted. During the voyage to Rosyth she would have no power whatsoever and her skeleton crew of 14 Swan Hunter riggers, commanded by Captain Frank McNulty, would be entirely dependent on the three tugs, *Beamish*, *Hendon* and *George V*, which were to carry out the tow.

The *Albion's* first journey to the open sea began on the morning of Monday 17 October 1949 when she was towed down the River Tyne and into the North Sea. The voyage did not get off to a good start for, two miles off Tynemouth, the *Albion* struck and set adrift a wreck marker buoy. However, as no damage was caused to the carrier, the slow journey north continued but, with weather conditions deteriorating, it was clear that it was not going to be an easy trip.

That evening, as darkness fell, severe south-easterly gales blew up and the three tugs got into difficulties with the

GEORGE V   HENDON   BEAMISH

Albion under tow in the North Sea on 17 October 1949 and on her way to Rosyth for docking. She has no island superstructure and the lift wells are open to the weather. In the early hours of the following morning she was involved in the tragic collision with the collier *Maystone*.

helpless carrier which, at times, was drifting out of control. As the severe storms, with winds in excess of 85mph, swept the north-east coast, the 2,000-ton collier *Maystone*, owned by the Thomas Stone Shipping Co of Swansea and manned by a crew of 25, was struggling south. She had left the port of Methil during the afternoon of 17 October with a cargo of coal for the Deptford Power Station on the River Thames. At 4.15am on Tuesday 18 October, with the *Maystone* and the *Albion* about four miles north-east of the Longstone Lighthouse on the Farne Islands, Third Officer John Louden on the *Maystone* experienced a severe jolt and heard the sound of grinding metal. Mr Louden was horrified to see that the *Maystone* was directly beneath the after overhang, on the port side, of an aircraft-carrier and that his vessel was sinking rapidly. The Master of the *Maystone*, Captain J. H. Williams, barely had time to order 'abandon ship' before the collier sank, leaving the crew struggling in the water. On board the *Albion* the collision had been felt only as a gentle bump, but fortunately those on watch at the stern of the carrier knew what had happened and they were able to throw lines to the men in the water. Three members of the collier's crew were pulled to safety and a fourth, who did not have the strength to

climb up the rope he was holding on to, was rescued by one of the *Albion's* crew members who bravely climbed down a lifeline with a rope which he was able to secure around the waist of the collier's last survivor. Despite a great deal of effort by the *Albion's* crew, who had to work by the light of oil lamps and hand torches, they were unable to rescue any more of the *Maystone's* crew and a thorough search by the Holy Island lifeboat failed to find any trace of more survivors. The collier had sunk in less than 15 minutes and in those stormy seas there was no hope of finding anyone else alive.

Although the *Albion* had also been damaged by the collision and had a 15ft hole aft on the port side, she was not in any immediate danger of sinking. However, with five feet of water in the engine-room and with the ship still taking in water, it was clear that she had to be brought to safety as soon as possible. During the forenoon of Tuesday 18 October the severe south-easterly gales continued and the *Albion's* progress north was painfully slow. Then, that afternoon, the winds changed direction and the carrier was swept towards the coast. As the tugs attempted to tow her into shallow waters in case she foundered, the *Hendon* got a wire hawser wrapped round her propeller shaft and she was disabled. An urgent request for assistance was sent to Rosyth and with the *Albion* virtually hove to and with water still pouring into her damaged hull, it was thought that the carrier might be lost.

However, soon afterwards the winds eased temporarily, and the destroyer *St James*, which was already at sea, arrived to assist the disabled tug *Hendon*. The next vessel to reach the scene was the Admiralty tug *Restive* and as soon as the *Hendon's* propeller was cleared, all four tugs, with the *St James* standing by, took up the tow once again. That night progress was slow and at daybreak on 19 October the *Albion* was still 15 miles east of the Forth Bridge. Fortunately there were no further problems and at 1pm that day the *Albion* dropped anchor one mile east of the bridge. Five hours later she was berthed at Rosyth Dockyard and the next morning she was dry docked without incident.

It was March 1953 before litigation over the tragic sinking of the *Maystone* was concluded and the Court of Appeal ruled that two-thirds of the blame should be apportioned to the *Albion's* builders, Swan Hunter & Wigham Richardson and one-third to the tug owners, France Fenwick & Co. It was also ruled that there was no evidence of negligence on the part of the *Maystone*. It was held that the defective port navigation light was a contributory cause of the collision, as was the failure to use 'not under command' lights. In view of the atrocious weather which had been forecast, the court also criticized the decision to put to sea at all on that fateful morning of Monday 17 October 1949.

It had been a tragic and traumatic voyage and, for the *Albion*, an inauspicious start to her career.

Albion's first full power trial in the North Sea in June 1953 during her builder's trials. At this stage the angled deck had not been constructed.

Chapter Two

The New Carrier

Following repairs to the collision damage and with the scraping and repainting of her underwater hull completed, the *Albion's* journey back to Swan Hunter's shipyard at Wallsend passed without incident and by the spring of 1950 work was well under way.

During the early months of 1953 a number of key officers were appointed to the ship and her first Supply Officer, Commander Ian Hamilton RN, received his appointment on 17 February. This is how he recalls those early days: 'I had but a vague idea of what would be required of me. I knew that, eventually, I would be involved in storing the ship and organizing the issue of stores, clothing and victualling, as well as making arrangements for the pay office records and cyphering, but initially it was difficult to imagine what duties I would have to undertake during the building stage. Somehow I thought I would be given plans and blueprints, and that I would be required to ensure that the builders were complying with these to the letter. The ship, at that time, was more or less still a hulk. Each evening, when the workmen had finished, the electricity supply to the *Albion* was cut off and she was in darkness.

On the morning of my arrival at the yard I was informed that a preliminary inspection of the Warrant Officers' galley would be carried out and, during the inspection, I would be accompanied by a Warrant Officer from the staff of the Admiral Superintendent. Imagine my surprise when I was told that I had to decide exactly where all the fittings and equipment for the galley were to be placed. All went well until I suggested that a working space was so narrow that the cooks would have difficulty passing each other with hot pans when the ship might be pitching and rolling. The Warrant Shipwright immediately suggested that we take the offending bulkhead back "a foot or two". What that extra space eventually cost the taxpayer I do not know but, as Swan Hunter were being paid an extra percentage over and above the contract price, there was no difficulty in getting the work done.

A similar procedure was followed in respect of all the other compartments for which I was responsible and, against my better judgement, I followed the advice of an "expert" from the Director of Victualling and permitted the food hot-lockers at the galley serving hatches to be fitted at such a height that would prevent the cooks, when swabbing the tiled decks, from accidentally pushing pieces of waste under them, but not high enough to enable any dust and debris to be cleared out easily. This resulted, prior to captain's rounds, in the cooks having to lie down on their stomachs in order to extract by hand the waste material which had accumulated. The Chief Cook then had to do the same in order to ensure the job had been done properly and then I had to lie down and inspect the areas with my torch in order to check that the Chief Cook

The *Albion* arrives at Rosyth during her builder's trials. *(FAAM)*

On 25 May 1954 the main body of the *Albion's* ship's company join the ship at Newcastle upon Tyne. *(FAAM)*

had not missed anything. Now and again even the Captain too assumed this prone position in order to search for an "errant chip" which, if discovered, was apt to raise his blood pressure.

This free-for-all in the positioning of equipment had its disadvantages. One department would conscientiously try to avoid fitting their equipment close to a bulkhead door, in order to permit free access, whilst another department, when searching for space, would find these clear areas ideal for fitting their equipment. However, great credit was due to Swan Hunter for the way they fitted out the *Albion.'*

On 1 July 1953 Captain G. H. Beale RN, the carrier's first commanding officer, was appointed to the ship, although he and all the naval personnel worked from offices in the Swan Hunter buildings. Commander Hamilton recalls that Captain Beale lunched with the directors of Swan Hunter while he and the other Heads of Department lunched with the various managers at the yard. He recalls that it was a surprisingly formal affair: '...we always sat down at 1pm and rose at 2pm precisely. In the early days a few officers went to a local pub and they did not arrive for lunch until about ten minutes after the deadline. A "frosty" silence of disapproval ensued and after

that their arrival was always prompt.'

Commander Hamilton recalls that none of the stores whether naval, victualling or air department, were supplied automatically by the Admiralty but everything had to be requisitioned. As he points out: 'To give an idea of what this entailed just consider the provisions and cutlery required for 1,400 men. In addition to that, the galley equipment, the cleaning materials, the timber required by the shipwrights, sheet metal and tubes by the engine-room artificers and the spare pressure gauges and lagging needed in the engine-room department. Consider too the air stores - about 20,000 different items, the absence of any one of which might put a whole squadron of aircraft out of action. Taking all that into account it will be realized, I am sure, that I did not lose any sleep when the ship's chaplain visited my office one day to inform me that he was "very concerned" that the kneeling cushions for the ship's chapel had not arrived.'

Commander Hamilton also remembers that there were no facilities at the builder's yard for the storage of items which had been received and which were waiting to be stowed safely on board. 'A disused factory in Newcastle was rented and it was manned day and night by members of

The Commissioning Ceremony took place at 3.45pm on 26 May 1954. Here Captain Beale is seen arriving in the hangar where the ship's company are mustered. *(FAAM)*

the Naval Stores staff. This was a popular job, partly due, I believe, to the fact that those undertaking it had the company of locally acquired girl-friends.'

In June 1953 the *Albion* was ready to undertake her Contractors' Sea Trials as she was due to commission later that same summer. By that time work had almost been completed and the *Albion* was very similar in appearance to the earlier Colossus class of light fleet carriers of which she was in effect, an improved version.

Commander Hamilton remembers these trials when the *Albion* steamed under her own power to Rosyth where she was dry docked once again. 'I can recall that we had a minor disaster only a few days prior to sailing for Rosyth to undertake the builder's trials. The ship was to make the voyage under her own steam and so she was fuelled beforehand in preparation for the voyage north. In order to prevent airlocks in a pipe which ran through the main naval store, a cap was temporarily removed and then, unfortunately, left unattended whilst fuelling took place. Later that afternoon, when it was reported to me that the naval store was under two inches of thick, black furnace oil I thought someone was trying to "take the mickey". Unfortunately it was no joke, but Swan Hunter provided oilskins, rubber boots, gloves, shovels and brushes, together with a team of their own men to supplement the Naval Stores staff. Everyone worked hard and did a marvellous cleaning job and it seemed that every drop of oil had been removed. However, it is impossible to get rid of that type of thick oil completely and later, in the Mediterranean when the temperature in the compartment rose considerably, the foul-smelling black oil used to seep out from behind shelving and from between the seams in the corticene deck.'

Even after the *Albion* got under way a few more minor problems arose, as Commander Hamilton recalls: 'One evening in June 1953, after dark, we left the Tyne bound for Rosyth. The timing, of course, was in order that we could catch a tide, but the Tyne pilot was rather inebriated and he became a liability. Very early on in the voyage north he peered ahead from the navigation bridge and cried agitatedly, "Breakers ahead, breakers ahead!" In fact he was looking at canvas covers which had been rigged to protect the catapults at the forward end of the flight deck, and which were flapping in the breeze. He was escorted to a seat in the plot room and he took no further part in the proceedings.'

After carrying out full power trials in those very waters where, four years previously, she had been involved in the tragic collision with the *Maystone* and had lain almost helpless at the mercy of the elements, the *Albion* arrived at Rosyth for the second time in her career and was dry docked once again. This time as well as maintenance on the underwater hull, heeling trials were carried out, and at the conclusion of these three weeks later, she returned to the River Tyne.

On 31 August 1953, soon after she had arrived back at the builder's yard, Lieutenant-Commander Bernard C. Lyons RN, Lt-Cdr (Flying), was appointed to the *Albion* and he has vivid memories of that day: 'When I first arrived at Swan's jetty I can recall that the *Albion* was a rusty, dirty, towering hulk, complete with engines of course and, with the whole ship echoing to the sound of windy hammers, it was very noisy on board. My main memories are of a close-knit and enthusiastic team and, initially, we had a relaxed routine as we worked out watch-bills and

27 May 1954 and *Albion* is towed down the Tyne towards the open sea.

Tynesiders watch the new aircraft-carrier as she passes The Groyne, South Shields, on her way to the North Sea. She is still flying the Red Ensign at her stern.

routines which were necessary for the running of a large ship. However, as the pressure of work increased our hours became longer.'

On 24 September 1953, 350 miles away, at Dover, the Barons of the Cinque Ports held their 'Courts of Brotherhood and Guestling', and after the mayors of the Cinque Ports had undertaken the ancient ritual of their procession between the Maison Dieu, adjoining Dover Town Hall, and the Parish Church, the *Albion* was formally adopted by the Confederation. It was a link which would last until the ship's final weeks in commission 19 years later.

The *Albion* and her two sister ships *Bulwark* and *Centaur* had been designed in the early 1940s to operate piston-engined aircraft, but in the ten years which had passed since those early days great progress had been made in naval aviation and it was clear that all three ships would be operating much heavier, jet aircraft such as the Sea Venom and the Sea Hawk. Two important British innovations during those post-war years which made for easier operating of these aircraft were the angled flight deck, which rendered obsolete the crash barriers, and the mirror landing sight which took the place of the landing signals officer who waved 'bats' in order to guide incoming aircraft. In August 1953 the Admiralty decided to include these developments in the *Albion* and asked the builders to provide quotations and specifications for the work which would provide the ship with a $5\frac{1}{2}°$ 'interim angled deck'. In the event the cost was £50,000 and on 28 October 1953 work began to cut down the port sheerstrake and to resite the port walkways and the port forward Bofors, together with their directors. Lt-Cdr Lyons can recall a constant stream of orders for alterations and extras being received from the Admiralty but, on Swan's insistence, this ceased shortly before the building work was completed.

In addition to the technical innovations the *Albion*, and her sister ships, were also up to date as regards the living quarters for the ships' companies. In place of hammocks on the mess-decks there were tubular steel and canvas bunks, and the traditional mess-deck eating arrangements were replaced by a cafeteria system in spacious dining halls which were adjacent to the galley serving hatches. There was a fully equipped laundry which was capable of washing, drying and ironing all the men's clothing each week, and the NAAFI was equipped with the most modern ice-cream plant available. Commander Hamilton recalls that the wardroom was very favourably commented on by US Navy officers from the American carrier, USS *Randolph*, whose own facilities were much more austere.

It was May 1954 before work on the *Albion* was finally completed and as Lt-Cdr Lyons recalls: 'As Commissioning Day approached work on board got more hectic. More and more officers and ratings joined the ship and, by this time, the furniture was going aboard and workmen swarmed over the whole vessel. Until three or four days before the actual ceremony the ship was still in a very dirty, shabby condition and it appeared that she would never be ready on time. However, the builders imposed a moratorium, with none of us being allowed to set foot on board, and a huge army of cleaning ladies then "descended" on the ship. They cleaned, honed, painted and polished, so that by Commissioning Day she was spotlessly clean, glistening with new paint and looking very smart indeed. The ladies did quite a splendid job.'

During the afternoon of Tuesday 25 May 1954 the main body of the *Albion's* ship's company arrived at Carville Station, Wallsend, after travelling by train from Portsmouth. From the station the 315 ratings marched through the crowd-lined streets of Wallsend to the ship where, as they embarked, each man was provided with a card which showed his mess-deck, dining hall, sleeping berth, division, part of watch and action station. Members of the advance party, who were familiar with the ship, were detailed off to show them how to find, and to attend to, more urgent matters such as the heads, mess-decks and, of course, the dining area.

The Commissioning Service took place at 3.40pm the next day, 26 May 1954, when the lower deck was cleared and everyone mustered in the hangar for the service of dedication which was conducted by the Archdeacon of Northumberland, The Ven C. H. Ritchie MA, who was, in fact, the Chaplain to Her Majesty The Queen. During the service Swan Hunter's Works Band accompanied the hymn singing, and the Commissioning Warrant and the lesson were read by Captain Beale.

That evening there was a great deal of work to be done as more stores were embarked, while the managers, foremen and chargehands of Swan Hunter's work-force were suitably entertained, and the final preparations were made to get the vessel ready for sea. The following morning at 7.55am Special Sea Dutymen were called to their stations and 35 minutes later, with tugs secured forward and aft, the last lines were slipped and the *Albion* was heading for the open sea. Lt-Cdr Bernard Lyons recalls the occasion: 'Our slow passage down the river was like a "triumphal progress", with all the vessels which were alongside the various yards sounding their sirens. Both sides of the river bank were crowded with spectators to see the *Albion*, which was still flying the Red Ensign, make her way to the open sea.'

It had been ten years since the first keel plates had been laid for yard number 1721 but, at last, the new carrier was putting to sea.

Chapter Three

The First Commission - Mediterranean Fleet

Under her own power and with her own ship's company aboard, the *Albion* passed Tynemouth at 9.51am on Thursday 27 May 1954 and, after casting off the escorting tugs, she commenced her engine trials in the North Sea. That afternoon the ship was put through her paces at full power and at 9.12pm, with the acceptance trials satisfactorily completed, HMS *Albion* was accepted into Her Majesty's service. The Red Ensign was lowered and the White Ensign was broken at the peak. Soon afterwards the Swan Hunter trials personnel were disembarked off Tynemouth and the *Albion* set course for Portsmouth by way of the Pentland Firth.

At 1am the next day she passed close to the Longstone Light, the scene of her tragic collision almost four and a half years earlier. By 5.30pm that evening she was off Dunnett Head and at 5pm on Sunday 30 May she passed Lizard Point, after which she made for Spithead, where she anchored at 8.30am on Monday 31 May 1954, remaining there for three days. At 6.30am on 3 June she weighed anchor and started two weeks of sea trials. Each evening the ship returned to her Spithead anchorage and this intensive routine was only broken on Friday 18 June when, at 4pm, *Albion* anchored just west of the breakwater at Dover. For the first time since their departure from the Tyne leave was granted to the ship's company and Captain Beale called on the town's mayor and other civic dignitaries as the *Albion* made her first courtesy visit to the town which had adopted her. The following evening the ship played host to the Cinque Ports' dignitaries and there was an official cocktail party on board. The guests included the Governor of Dover Castle, Major-General H. F. S. King CB CBE MBE, who arrived on board in full mess dress. Commander Hamilton recalls the occasion which caused some amusement amongst the *Albion's* officers, as General King's epaulettes, which carried his badges of rank, were missing from his uniform. However, the Captain of Marines lent his 'shoulder-pips' to the General, who consequently spent the rest of the evening as a Royal Marines Captain. Fortunately, on the following day, Sunday 20 June, everything was in order when Major-General King visited the ship again to inspect Divisions on the flight deck.

The *Albion* left Dover at 10.15pm that evening and returned to Spithead where preparations were made to start her flying trials. She sailed during the afternoon of Thursday 24 June and after carrying out anti-submarine exercises she steamed to Milford Haven, where leave was granted and Lt-Cdr Parker RN, the CO of 898 Squadron

and other squadron personnel joined the ship. After a three-day visit to the port, which was also 'home' to many Fleet Air Arm squadrons, the *Albion* returned to Spithead and, at 12.18pm on Tuesday 29 June 1954, she made fast alongside Pitch House Jetty in Portsmouth Harbour for the first time.

During the six weeks she spent alongside Pitch House and Middle Slip Jetties, leave periods were granted to the ship's company, and the port Deck Landing Mirror Sight and radar equipment was embarked and fitted, and catapult trials were carried out which tested the catapults for the first time. Lt-Cdr Lyons recalls these vividly: 'They were called deadload trials and a load-carrying wheeled container, which was appropriately nicknamed "Dumbo", and which looked like a railway goods wagon, was used. "Dumbo's" weight was adjusted to correspond with the various aircraft which would be operated and floats were fitted to the contraption before it was launched over the bows. These tests were quite dramatic and they certainly caused some concern on board a flotilla of Portuguese frigates and minesweepers which were moored forward of us, as "Dumbo" splashed down some distance forward of the *Albion* and not far from them. After several shots from each catapult the tests were adjudged successful.'

Portsmouth's Navy Days that year were held on 31 July and the first two days of August, and the *Albion*, together with the battleship *Vanguard*, which was the flagship of the Home Fleet, stole the show.

The *Albion* left Portsmouth on 12 August 1954 and after completing speed trials off the measured mile at Portland, and having jackstay as well as RAS exercises, the ship was ready to start her flying trials, which subsequently took place in the Channel between the Isle of Wight and Portland Bill.

'Hands to Flying Stations' was piped for the first time at 9.15am on Monday 23 August 1954 and in the half-hour which followed a piston-engined Avenger, flown by Lt-Cdr J. H. B. Bedells RN of the Service Trials Unit (STU), made the first deck landing. Later in the day both Sea Hawk and Skyraiders of 898 and 849 Squadrons respectively landed on. All next day the flying trials, involving Avengers, Sea Hawks, Skyraiders and Gannet aircraft continued without incident, but at just after 1pm on Wednesday 25 August, the ship's first fatal accident occurred.

The *Albion* was just south of the Isle of Wight and as part of her catapult and arrester gear trials she was carrying out a number of launches with Gannet aircraft of the STU from RAE Farnborough. At about 1.15pm a Gannet

At 9.51 am on 27 May 1954 *Albion* reached the open waters of the North Sea where the tugs cast off and the ship started her acceptance trials.

Deadload trials at Portsmouth in early July 1954. 'Dumbo' is loaded onto the port catapult... *(FAAM)*

...and gives the Portuguese Navy a fright. HMS *Centaur* can be seen ahead of the Portuguese ships at Middle Slip Jetty. *(FAAM)*

The DH 110 piloted by Lt-Cdr 'Jock' Elliot RN makes one of a number of 'touch and go' circuits. It was the first time that the aircraft had operated on a carrier's flight deck. *(FAAM)*

piloted by Lt-Cdr A. D. Cassidi RN*, the CO of 820 Sqdn, with a civilian, Mr P. A. Byrne of the RAE as observer, was launched off the starboard catapult. Although it appeared in every respect to be a perfectly satisfactory launch, the aircraft lost power, slewed to starboard, then stalled from about 10ft and dropped nose down into the sea. Within 30 seconds of it having hit the water it was fully submerged, and although the SAR helicopter was on the scene in less than one minute, its crew were only able to rescue the pilot. There was no sign of the observer. A subsequent Board of Inquiry found that the pilot had no time to warn his passenger that they were about to ditch, and being completely unprepared with his hood closed, he had been unable to escape.

After searching the area for several hours, the flying trials continued later that afternoon and Sea Venoms carried out their first deck landings. On 26 August 1954 the Minister of Supply, Mr Duncan Sandys, embarked by helicopter to watch the day's flying trials and on 29 August a variety of shore-based aircraft carried out 'wire pulling' exercises. The aircraft were known as 'clockwork mice' and the object was to land on each aircraft with arrests being made by each of the *Albion's* six arrester wires.

On the last day of August the *Albion* anchored at Spithead and on the following day she steamed into Portsmouth Harbour and was secured alongside Middle Slip Jetty. Two weeks later, on 13 September 1954, she put to sea once again and, after carrying out heeling trials, she steamed west for the mouth of the Bristol Channel where she embarked her Sea Hawks of 898 Squadron and Wyverns of 813 Squadron. There then followed six days of intensive flying exercises, at the completion of which the ship would moor each day in Portland Harbour. On Thursday 23 September, having embarked 44 Press representatives, *Albion* left Portland at just after 9am, and made history when, at noon, after a busy morning's flying exercises, a sonic boom announced the arrival of a DH 110, (the prototype of the De Havilland Sea Vixen), piloted by Lt-Cdr 'Jock' Elliot RN from Boscombe Down. After making a circuit of the new carrier and a low, slow run over the flight deck, Lt-Cdr Elliot went on to execute a number of 'touch and go' circuits from *Albion's* flight deck. It was the aircraft's first landing on an aircraft-carrier, although the *Albion* would never carry them herself. During the late afternoon of Saturday 25 September *Albion* anchored at Spithead and leave was granted. With her

*Later Admiral Sir A. D. Cassidi GCB

Skyraiders of 849 C Flight over the *Albion*.

The *Albion* at Portland during her work-up. The Sea Hawks of 898 Squadron are lined up on the flight deck and the Z on their tails indicates that they are *Albion's* aircraft.

A Skyraider lands on. *(FAAM)*

Catapulting Sea Hawks.
(FAAM)

Albion returns to Portland during her work-up.

initial shakedown trials successfully completed, she was ready for foreign service.

At 9.30am on Wednesday 29 September 1954, *Albion* weighed anchor and left Spithead bound for Gibraltar and the Mediterranean Fleet where she would join her sister ship *Centaur*. On her way south through the Bay of Biscay *Albion* took part in her first NATO exercise, 'Morning Mist', which was designed to test convoy escorts in the Channel and the Western Approaches. Fortunately it was only an exercise for 'hostile' submarines jubilantly announced that they had twice 'torpedoed' and finally 'sunk' a large merchant ship off Ushant. The merchantman was, in fact, the *Albion* which had been injected into the exercise to represent an independently routed troop transport. However, her minor role in the exercise having been completed, and with air and sea temperatures rising,

Captain Beale was able to stop the ship off the Portuguese coast and pipe, 'hands to bathe'.

Early in the morning of Tuesday 5 October 1954 the *Albion* was secured starboard side alongside 47 berth of Gibraltar's South Mole and once the formalities of the gun salutes were completed, leave was granted to the ship's company. While they enjoyed the Mediterranean sunshine during this seven-day stop-over, the Gibraltar Dockyard completed necessary work to the starboard mirror sight and the flight deck was painted in pastel green and grey, intersected by various yellow, white and red lines.

It was then time to move on and at just before 8am on Tuesday 12 October 1954, *Albion* slipped her berth and set courses east for Malta. The following morning, in a position Lat 35°- 50'N/Long 4° - 59'W, 'flying stations' was piped. Soon after flying operations started that day a

An Avenger takes off from the port catapult.

Wyvern, piloted by Lieutenant Bruce Macfarlane RN, experienced a 'flame out' whilst going off the port catapult and then plunged into the sea. It hit the water almost under the ship's bows, was rammed by the carrier and sank immediately. Lt Macfarlane's remarkable escape is best told in his own words: 'Catapulting is a somewhat startling experience and I personally am just about off the bows before I collect my wits enough to be aware of anything and take control of the aircraft. In this case my first realization was loss of power; I tried to open the throttle, but this was already locked in the open position. The next instant I hit the sea, I suppose at about 70 knots, wheels down and flaps in take-off position. I knew that Wyvern aircraft had extremely bad ditching characteristics and I had, in fact, witnessed a fatal ditching some 18 months earlier. This memory flashed through my mind just before I hit the sea and I felt that I had no chance of escape. The impact with the sea stunned me to some extent.

When I had collected my wits again I was under water and it was getting darker. I had one thought; to get out of the aircraft. My nervous state seemed to disconnect my body from my brain - except for my left hand. The yellow emergency canopy jettison knob filled my whole vision. I was grateful for its colour and position. I hit it with my left hand and the canopy became unlocked and green water poured in all round the edges. I did not notice the canopy

actually go and it may have been still more or less in position when I ejected. I pulled the blind handle with my left hand only, immediately after hitting the hood jettison lever.

I was wearing a crash helmet and the actual ejection seemed identical to that on the test rig. I pulled the firing handle, nothing happened and I knew that I had to pull it a little further. I was fired out, and blacked out momentarily, the next awareness being that I was out of the aircraft. I have no way of knowing, but imagine that I was ejected at about ten to 20ft below the surface, with the aircraft in about a 30° nose-down position. In any case ejection did not bring me to the surface.

I only learnt later that after the aircraft entered the sea the bows of the ship hit it and cut the rear fuselage in two; the tail and a collapsed fuselage fuel tank were seen from the helicopter to pass down the starboard side of the ship. I assume I was out before the ship hit the aircraft as I was not aware of any impact shock.

As soon as I collected my wits again after ejection, I was aware of being tumbled violently over and over in the light green sea and becoming tangled in the seat. I saw yellow nylon by my face, presumably the drogue 'chute fired automatically from the seat. I had choked in quite a lot of water by this time and the drowning aspect was no longer unpleasant, but very like drinking fresh water.

During this head over heels tumbling in the ship's wake, or possibly under the ship, I must have undone my parachute straps, though I have no clear memory of this. Probably at this time too I lost my crash helmet and inner flying helmet and, perhaps, oxygen mask. Anyway, when I finally surfaced I did not have these items.

Eventually the tumbling ceased and I thought I was going to live and then, to my bitter disappointment, I began to be dragged slowly down, deeper and deeper. I must have reached an advanced stage of drowning as I was in a dreamy, relaxed, comfortable, but sad state, slowly "floating" deeper. I had given up the struggle.

Suddenly all the tangle freed itself, a spark of life reached my brain, but the dinghy lanyard was still pulling me down. I followed my hand down and fumbled twice with the release catch and undid it. Then I began rising. For the first time I now had a very desperate need for air; I tried to swim upwards. I suddenly remembered my Mae West, and to help me reach the surface as quickly as possible I inflated it, and popped upwards like a cork into the sunshine.'

Fortunately Lt Macfarlane was quickly picked up by the plane-guard helicopter and, despite his harrowing experience, a broken collar bone, abrasions and bruises, he managed to produce a broad grin when he was delivered back on board. However, as a precaution, it was decided not to catapult any more Wyvern aircraft until the reason for the 'flame out' had been investigated. Flying operations continued during the afternoon of Wednesday 13 October with pilots of 898 Squadron and 849 C Flight agreeing

A Sea Hawk lands on.

Albion arrives in Grand Harbour to join the Mediterranean Fleet. *(FAAM)*

On 25 October 1954, Admiral Lord Mountbatten, C-in-C Mediterranean Fleet, visited the ship. Here he is seen meeting the Heads of Department.
(FAAM)

Albion in the Mediterranean with Sea Hawks, Wyverns and Skyraiders ranged on deck.
(FAAM)

Ranging Skyraiders, Sea Hawks and Wyverns. *(FAAM)*

A US Navy Cougar from USS *Lake Champlain* practises 'touch and go' circuits.
(FAAM)

that the new flight deck colour scheme was a great help when landing.

On 16 October, with the ship off Malta, all the Wyvern aircraft of 813 Squadron were flown off to Hal Far and the *Albion* anchored in Marsaxlokk Bay off the south-east tip of the island. Three days later at 9.30am on Tuesday 19 October, after firing a 17-gun salute to the C-in-C Mediterranean Fleet, Admiral The Earl Mountbatten of Burma, the *Albion* passed through the breakwater to berth in Grand Harbour.

During the morning of Monday 25 October 1954 Lord Mountbatten visited the ship and, after meeting all the Heads of Department, he addressed the ship's company. Next morning, having hoisted the flag of Flag Officer, Aircraft-Carriers (FOAC), Rear-Admiral W. T. Couchman CVO DSO DSC*, the *Albion* left Grand Harbour for a week of intensive exercises which would put the ship through its paces and prepare her for joint exercises with both the US Sixth Fleet and the Italian Navy. On one day alone 898 Squadron and 849 C Flight managed to achieve 50 sorties, which called for a great deal of hard work by both aircrews and handling parties.

Thursday 4 November saw the *Albion* back at No 7 buoy in Grand Harbour where the FOAC transferred his flag to *Centaur*. Since her flying trials had started on 23 August, 537 catapult launches and 775 arrested deck landings, including 513 mirror landings, had been

achieved. In addition to this commendable score, since her commissioning some 322 helicopter landings had been recorded. It was a very impressive start.

On 11 November 1954, *Albion* slipped her mooring in Grand Harbour and put to sea. She was now a fully fledged member of the Mediterranean Fleet and after embarking 803 Sea Hawk Squadron she joined up with the *Centaur* for further flying exercises. These were marred by two fatal accidents, the first at 9.25am on Tuesday 16 November, when Leading Airman Darbyshire, who was employed on flight deck duties, was hit by a Sea Hawk which skidded off the flight deck whilst landing. That afternoon, shortly before both carriers anchored in Marsaxlokk Bay, the funeral service was held and the body of L/A Darbyshire was committed to the deep. Six more days of exercises with the *Centaur* followed before, at 3.46am on Tuesday 23 November *Albion* left Marsaxlokk Bay, bound for Naples and a six-day visit. However, only hours after sailing, at 6.35am and in a position Lat 36° - 01'N/Long 15° - 17'E, the second fatal accident took place.

'Flying Stations' had been sounded at 6.30am and the first event of the day was to be the launching of eight Sea Hawks of 898 Squadron. The first six of these took place without incident, but when the turn came for the seventh aircraft in the range, piloted by Lieutenant Allan R. Wright RN, problems were encountered. The facts, as related by Captain Beale in his report to FOAC, best describe the events which led to the tragic and inexplicable accident which followed. 'The seventh aircraft, piloted by Lt Wright, arrived at the catapult ready position where he was shown the cockpit check board. The aircraft was stopped here by a director, after he had faced it towards the port catapult. All signals given by this director were obeyed by Lt Wright and everything appeared perfectly normal. When the port catapult was clear Lt Wright was passed to the director standing astride the catapult track. The aircraft taxied onto the loading chocks in the normal manner and there came to rest after being centralized.

The holdback number operated the quick release gear and the holdback dropped into position in the fish tail of the holdback leader. At this stage the loading chocks would normally have been lowered by a signal from the Flight Deck Engineer Officer but, owing to the fact that the retraction of the starboard catapult shuttle had cut in on the retraction of the port shuttle causing a temporary halt in its retraction, the Flight Deck Engineer Officer delayed lowering the loading chocks while he investigated the reason for the shuttle delay. When, however, a moment or two later

he saw both shuttles retract, he gave the signal to the port catapult operator to lower the loading chocks. This delay resulted in the aircraft remaining in position against the loading chocks for an appreciably longer time than usual.

Because of the noise emanating from the eighth aircraft being loaded onto the starboard catapult, it cannot be definitely established whether the pilot had excessive power settings on the aircraft while in position against the loading chocks. It is, however, certain that when the loading chocks were lowered on the signal from the Flight Deck Engineer Officer, the pilot had released the brakes and the engine was running at nearly full power, if not actually at full power.

This caused the aircraft to leap forward, shock loading the resilient loader and causing a fracture of the break-out ring. The aircraft then mounted the safety chocks, port wheel first, and moved towards the bows. The towing pendant had not been attached.

The Captain of the flight deck who was directing the aircraft had given the "off brakes" signal when he saw the loading chocks lowered. His normal signal would then have been "come forward", to tension the holdback in the

Wyverns and Sea Hawks parked forward of the island. The angled flight deck allowed flying operations to continue.

(FAAM)

Mediterranean Sea October 1954, a Skyraider of 849 C Flight landing on.

January 1955, catapulting Sea Hawks.

A magnificent view of the *Albion* in the Mediterranean sunshine. *(FAAM)*

Sea Hawks starting up. *(FAAM)*

Sea Hawks being catapulted. *(FAAM)*

A Sea Hawk mishap. *(FAAM)*

Albion approaches Grand Harbour's breakwater.

holdback loader. However, on seeing the aircraft bound forward over the safety chocks he did not give this signal but did, in fact, give the "emergency stop" signal. This he continued to do in an urgent manner until the aircraft's forward motion forced him to jump to one side.

The Flight Deck Officer had turned towards the port catapult after launching the sixth aircraft from the starboard catapult at just about the moment that Lt Wright's aircraft surged forward. He ran beside the aircraft for a short distance waving his red flag and then stopped, expecting the pilot to take the necessary corrective action and certain in his own mind that he would do so. The aircraft, however, continued up the flight deck at a brisk walking pace with no apparent alteration in power setting, until it toppled over the bows.'

The pilot of the planeguard helicopter, who witnessed the whole incident, saw Lt Wright's aircraft hit the water, still in a level position between 50 and 100 feet ahead of the ship, but the pilot did not make any attempt to escape before the *Albion's* bows struck the Sea Hawk, which then disappeared from his view down the port side. Despite the fact that, within seconds, the helicopter was over the sinking aircraft, they were unable to recover the pilot.

Meanwhile, the *Albion* herself was stopped and the seaboat was lowered, but, despite an extensive search of the area, there was no trace of the pilot or of any wreckage. That afternoon, as the ship continued her voyage to Naples, a memorial service was held for Lt Wright.

At 10am the next morning, after a full ceremonial entry into the harbour, the *Albion* tied up alongside the quay at Naples, in company with the destroyer HMS *Diana* and the US aircraft-carrier USS *Lake Champlain*. Following the successful six-day visit, the *Albion* left the Italian port to join the USS *Lake Champlain* and a number of Italian warships in 'Exercise Napolex'. On Thursday 2 December 1954, returning to Malta, she passed over the spot where only nine days earlier Lt Wright and his Sea Hawk had been tragically and inexplicably lost, and at 6.55am a wreath in his memory was dropped from the quarterdeck.

Following her return to the Malta area *Albion* took part in exercises with her sister ship *Centaur*, before entering Grand Harbour where, as was most often the case during her visits to the port, she moored at 11 berth, between RNH Bighi and Customs House Steps. The *Albion* was soon at sea again for local fleet exercises which took her south to within 20 miles of Tripoli. Then on the afternoon of Wednesday 15 December 1954 she docked again at 11 berth, Grand Harbour, in preparation for Christmas and the New Year. During her stay the C-in-C Mediterranean Fleet made an official visit and on Christmas Day there was a carol service in the hangar. On Boxing Day the ship was opened to visitors and both the ship's launches and the local dghajsas did a roaring trade, as did the countless bars in Strait Street, serving those who wished to take advantage of the dubious pleasures which 'The Gut' had to offer.

During her calls at Malta the ship's company displayed their prowess in inter-service events, particularly in the cross-country running where *Albion's* athletes swept all before them, including a Royal Marine Commandos team. At 9am on Monday 3 January 1955 Captain W. A. F. Hawkins DSO OBE DSC RN joined the ship from HMS *St Angelo* and assumed command from Captain Beale who was returning home to the UK and a well-earned retirement. At 11.25am, to the cheers of the ship's company, the Heads of Department rowed him from the *Albion* to Customs House Steps where he took leave of his final command.

Captain Hawkins took his new command to sea for the first time on Wednesday 12 January 1955 and for the following five days the ship carried out flying exercises in the waters off Malta. Lt-Cdr Bernard Lyons recalls that on occasions he would 'borrow' one of the Sea Hawks in order to get flying practice: 'It was a delightful aircraft to fly and the mirror sight was a great success and so easy to use. The view of the deck whilst landing a Sea Hawk was excellent and so unlike the piston-engined aircraft that I had previously flown from carriers. In those days the angled deck was a novel concept and a very successful one. It

At 11.25am on Monday 3 January 1955 *Albion's* first commanding officer, Captain G. H. Beale DSO OBE RN, was rowed ashore from the ship by the Heads of Department. He was returning home to retirement and Captain W. A. F. Hawkins RN assumed command.

(FAAM)

enabled pilots to practise deck landings and by keeping the arrester hook in the up position, it enabled them to take off again immediately they had touched down. Such 'touch and go' landings had previously been impossible. It also made the crash barrier a thing of the past, although *Albion's* barriers were still fitted.'

On Monday 16 January the *Albion* left Marsaxlokk Bay for Toulon, where she arrived for a four-day courtesy visit early in the morning of Thursday 20 January. Once again the visit was a great success, although the ship's cross-country running team missed the Mediterranean Fleet Championships which were held in Malta. The *Albion's* team had gained a formidable reputation and there were some who believed the event had been deliberately organized so that they would be excluded, being safely out of the way in Toulon.

On leaving Toulon the *Albion* rendezvoused with her sister ship *Centaur*, wearing the flag of FOAC, Rear-Admiral A. R. Pedder, and the two carriers joined vessels of the French Navy and the US Sixth Fleet. The latter consisted of the aircraft-carriers *Randolph* and *Lake Champlain*, the battleship *Iowa* and the cruiser *Northampton*, wearing the flag of Vice-Admiral T. S. Combs USN. For three days the combined fleet exercises concentrated on air defence and on 29 January Vice-Admiral Combs landed on board the *Albion* by helicopter to watch his Grumman Cougar aircraft land on the British carrier in cross-decking exercises, and to see for himself the angled deck and mirror landing aid in use. On Wednesday 2 February 1955, with the exercises completed, the *Albion* and *Centaur*, escorted by three US destroyers, set course for

Malta and the following day the squadrons were flown off to Hal Far. At 9am on Saturday 5 February the *Albion* was secured to No 13 buoy in Bighi Bay, Grand Harbour, for a nine-day self-maintenance period.

At 8.30am on Monday 14 February 1955 the *Albion* put to sea once more, this time for FOAC's sea inspection and, after re-embarking her squadrons, there followed three days of intensive flying exercises as Rear-Admiral Pedder put all departments through their paces. The inspection was followed by local fleet exercises off Malta before, on Wednesday 23 February, the *Albion* returned to Grand Harbour for a further 12 days of self maintenance, and a run ashore. Following this break she sailed again to participate in combined Mediterranean and Home Fleet exercises with the *Centaur*. During this period 845 Whirlwind Helicopter Squadron were embarked for 'Exercise Sea Lance' which involved putting Royal Marine Commandos ashore from an aircraft-carrier, which was a favourite project of the then C-in-C Mediterranean Fleet, Admiral Lord Mountbatten. It was almost a dummy run for *Albion's* future role. Following another seven-day stop-over in Grand Harbour, on the morning of Tuesday 22 March 1955 *Albion* slipped her berth once more, this time bound for Gibraltar and home. After embarking her squadrons once again, she joined the *Centaur* and the destroyer *Defender* for the voyage west. There followed only a brief 48-hour stop at Gibraltar before she set course for Portsmouth. On the last day of March 1955 the squadrons were flown off and the next day, to the great joy of the ship's company and their families, she tied up alongside Middle Slip Jetty in Portsmouth Dockyard.

A fine view of *Albion* as she manoeuvres. *(FAAM)*

31

Chapter Four

First Commission - East Of Suez

The *Albion's* first major refit lasted for over three months and during this time she spent most of May and ten days of June in dry dock. However, by Friday 5 July 1955 she was ready for sea once again and at 1.15pm that day she left Portsmouth Harbour to start her shakedown trials. The next ten days were full of activity as the various trials took place off Portland, but there was also time for some leisure, and on 11 July, between runs over the measured mile in Weymouth Bay, 'hands to bathe' was piped, which indicates it must have been a hot summer on the south coast! With her initial trials successfully completed, the *Albion* returned to Portsmouth during the afternoon of Friday 15 July and tied up alongside Pitch House Jetty for the weekend. On Monday 18 July she put to sea again, and the following day the squadrons flew on their aircraft. After landing on the Sea Venoms of 890 Squadron, the Avengers of 815 Squadron and the Skyraiders of 849 C Flight, five days of flying trials were held off Plymouth before courses were set for Ushant and

Gibraltar.

Following a short visit to Gibraltar and flying exercises off Malta, the *Albion* returned to Grand Harbour on Thursday 11 August 1955 for a three-day break, after which she left to rendezvous with HMS *Eagle* and units of the US Sixth Fleet, including the Midway-class carrier USS *Coral Sea*. Once again combined fleet exercises followed, during which one of 890 Squadron's Sea Venoms was lost, but fortunately, on this occasion the aircrew were recovered safely. A fly-past by both *Albion's* and *Eagle's* aircraft over the USS *Coral Sea* marked the end of the exercises, and both the British aircraft-carriers then left the Mediterranean for the cold waters of the North Sea and finally Invergordon.

By 12.30am on the morning of Tuesday 13 September 1955 *Albion* was off the Mull of Galloway and later that morning she and the *Eagle* joined ships of the Home Fleet, including the cruiser *Glasgow* and the destroyers *Decoy*, *Agincourt*, *Barrosa* and *Diana*. Also present were the US

A pilot's eye view of *Albion's* flight deck.

A magnificent aerial view of *Albion* with Sea Hawks and Sea Venoms ranged on deck. *(FAAM)*

A Sea Venom lands on. *(FAAM)*

Navy ships *Northampton* and *Smalley*. Next day all the vessels took part in exercises off Invergordon and on Friday 16 September both *Eagle* and *Albion* anchored in the Cromarty Firth, that famous stretch of water which has seen so many major units of the Royal Navy. The following day, at just after noon, HMS *Bulwark* and HMS *Centaur* arrived as the Home Fleet rendezvoused for a major exercise, 'Sea Mist', which was to take place off the Norwegian coast in the Trondheim area. This was the first occasion on which the three light fleet carriers had come together and they remained at the anchorage before leaving during the morning of Tuesday 20 September for the coast of Norway.

The NATO exercise, which commenced on 21 September, was essentially designed to test anti-submarine defences, and it got off to a lively start when, at 1.40pm, a Whirlwind helicopter being flown by 845 Squadron's CO ditched ahead of the fleet. Fortunately all three crew members were rescued by one of *Albion's* helicopters. Over the next two days intensive flying exercises were carried out by aircraft from all four carriers. At 9.50am on the morning of Tuesday 27 September a Dragonfly helicopter, which was leaving from *Bulwark*, ditched shortly after take-off and helicopters were scrambled on board both the *Bulwark* and the *Albion*. Fortunately, again there were no casualties with two survivors being picked up by *Bulwark's* helicopter and one by *Albion's*. The next day, Wednesday 28 September, after *Albion* had embarked 811 Sea Hawk Squadron, 'Sea Mist' was concluded and all four carriers dropped anchor at 6.15pm for a courtesy visit to Trondheim, and leave was granted. The first day of the visit started well with the carriers dressed overall in honour of HRH The Prince of Norway. At 9am launches started to

ferry liberty men ashore. However, by midday gale force winds were causing problems and the boat routine had to be suspended. At 3pm that afternoon, with wind speeds increasing and with the carriers in a very exposed anchorage, both the *Eagle* and *Bulwark* were forced to put to sea. Fortunately, in the early hours of the following morning the gales moderated and the boat service was resumed.

HMS *Albion* left Trondheim for Copenhagen early on the morning of Monday 3 October and she was joined by HMS *Apollo* wearing the flag of the C-in-C Home Fleet, Admiral Sir Michael Denny GCB CBE DSC, and by the two Daring-class destroyers, *Decoy* and *Diana*. After anchoring off the Skagen Light during the night, the ships made a full ceremonial entry into the Danish capital on the morning of Thursday 6 October and the *Albion* tied up alongside a berth at Langeline. That evening the C-in-C held a reception on board the *Albion* for his Danish counterpart and the Danish Chief of Staff and Defence Ministry officials. The next day thousands of the city's residents queued to visit the *Albion*, while the ship's company flocked ashore to sample the delights of the Tivoli Gardens. There was a particularly successful children's party on board, and after four hectic days, with happy memories all round and presumably with some empty wallets as well, the visit came to an end. For the voyage across the North Sea the *Albion* was escorted by a radar bedecked Soviet 'trawler' which saw her safely over to Rosyth. Later that month the *Albion*, again in company with *Bulwark*, *Centaur* and *Eagle*, took part in a NATO air defence exercise, 'Phoenix One', in the North Sea off the Skagerrak. During the exercise a Sea Hawk was lost when a huge wave broke over the ship's bow during take-off, but fortunately

HMS *Albion* arrives at Malta's Grand Harbour on 11 August 1955.

Albion floodlit at Copenhagen during her visit to the Danish port in October 1955. *(FAAM)*

Albion makes a ceremonial entry into Grand Harbour on 20 January 1956, shortly before leaving for South-East Asia.

Albion (in foreground) and the *Centaur* moored in Grand Harbour. *(FAAM)*

Albion refuels at sea during her Far Eastern deployment. *(FAAM)*

the pilot was rescued. The exercise was completed on Saturday 29 October and the following day saw all four carriers anchored at Rosyth once again.

The *Albion* left Rosyth on 1 November and three days later she was back alongside Middle Slip Jetty at Portsmouth where she was to prepare for the final leg of her commission.

With all aircraft-carriers under the direct command of FOAC, all the operational carriers generally rotated between the Mediterranean and Home Fleets, which had in fact been merged in many respects. The naval force maintained in the Far East was relatively small although, in order to demonstrate the mobility of naval power, aircraft-carriers were temporarily detached east of Suez. It was with this mobility in mind that it had been decided to send both the *Albion* and *Centaur* on a five-month tour of duty to the Far East. The detachment had two purposes, the first being to take part in tactical exercises with the Far East Fleet and the Australian and New Zealand Navies, and secondly to give a demonstration of naval flying to members of the Indian government who were known to be considering buying an aircraft-carrier for the Indian Navy.

For most of the ship's company the festive season of 1955 was spent at home with their families and at 9am on Tuesday 10 January 1956, Rear-Admiral A. R. Pedder, FOAC, hoisted his flag in the *Albion*, and exactly one hour

later she slipped from South Railway Jetty. At the same time the *Centaur* left Middle Slip Jetty and took station astern of the *Albion* as the two carriers left Portsmouth for their 'flag flying' tour east of Suez. After embarking their squadrons both vessels set courses for Ushant and after a short stop at Gibraltar they arrived in Malta during the afternoon of Friday 20 January. For the remainder of the month the two carriers remained in the Malta area carrying out various manoeuvres and exercises with HMS *Ark Royal*. On the morning of Monday 6 February both the *Albion* and the *Centaur* left Grand Harbour bound for Port Said. Weather conditions in the eastern Mediterranean at the time were bad and at 7pm that evening radio contact was lost with one of *Albion's* Gannets which had been taking part in a night-flying exercise. During the night a major search operation was launched by both the *Albion* and the *Centaur*, together with their escorting destroyer, HMS *Urania*, and an RAF Shackleton from Malta. At 2.30am on Tuesday 7 February *Centaur* had to break off and return to Malta with engine trouble but, despite severe snow storms, the search continued. Sadly no trace was found of the aircraft or its crew members and *Albion* and *Urania* resumed their voyage, arriving off Port Said during the afternoon of Thursday 9 February. They made their southbound transit of the Suez Canal the following day, and 24 hours later had entered the Red Sea. *Albion*, with her escort, arrived in Aden during the afternoon of Tuesday 14 February and it was during her 19-hour stop-over there that the *Centaur* joined her once again.

The two ships left Aden for Bombay at 7am on Wednesday 15 February 1956 and set courses across the Arabian Sea which offered a welcome relief after the stifling heat of the Red Sea and the anchorage off Steamer Point at Aden. Four days later, at 2.35pm on Sunday 19 February, while off the coast of India, *Albion* and *Centaur* rendezvoused with the Indian cruiser *Delhi* (ex-HMS *Achilles* of River Plate fame). After exchanging salutes, the remainder of that day, and the following day, were spent putting both carriers through their paces, and early on the morning of Tuesday 21 February the group rendezvoused with the Indian Navy frigates *Cauvery* and *Kistna* (ex-RN Black Swan class). On board the latter vessel were the Prime Minister of India, Mr Jawaharlal Nehru, and officials from the Indian Defence Ministry. After transferring to the *Albion*, Mr Nehru spent the day on board touring the ship and meeting Heads of Departments, after which he was treated to a demonstration of naval flying. By the time he disembarked by helicopter at 2.15pm, the *Centaur* had been detached to Karachi for her six-day official visit, and less than half an hour later the *Albion* anchored in Bombay Harbour, within a quarter of a mile of the 'Gateway to India'.

After a somewhat hectic six-day visit to Bombay, *Albion*, in company with INS *Delhi*, left the port and steamed south for Colombo where she arrived during the afternoon of Thursday 1 March 1956, and tied up to a buoy in the city's busy commercial harbour. During her four days at Colombo *Albion* enjoyed a constant stream of visitors, including various government ministers who were keen to look at the new carrier. Then at 9am on Monday 5 March she left for Singapore, and in the evening, after refuelling from RFA *Wave Master*, she rejoined the *Centaur* and destroyers of the Far East Fleet, including the *Cossack* and *Concord*, and the Australian destroyers *Anzac* and *Tobruk*. There then followed a five-day voyage across the Bay of Bengal before the two carriers sailed south through the Straits of Malacca to anchor off the Sultan Shoal on Singapore's south coast. Early next morning both ships weighed anchor and steamed round the east coast, past Changi to the Naval Base on the island's north coast. After a full ceremonial entry with salutes to the C-in-C Far East Station, the *Albion* was secured alongside No 14 berth. The first part of the Far Eastern voyage had been completed successfully and, in fact, talks were under way in Delhi between British and Indian defence officials which would result, within 12 months, in the Indian Navy buying the uncompleted Majestic-class aircraft-carrier *Hercules*. The vessel was subsequently reconstructed and modernized by Harland & Wolff at Belfast, before being commissioned into the Indian Navy as the *Vikrant*.

After only four days in the Naval Base at Singapore,

both the *Albion* and *Centaur* put to sea once again, this time bound for Hong Kong, in company with the cruiser *Newfoundland* which was wearing the flag of Vice-Admiral Sir Alan Scott-Moncrieff KCB CBE DSO, C-in-C Far East Station. During the four-day passage through the South China Sea the two carriers took part in night-flying exercises and at 2pm on Monday 19 March 1956 they moored at buoys in Hong Kong Harbour. During the remainder of that month both ships took part in an 'Anzam' exercise, 'Sea Dragon', in the South China Sea with the French aircraft-carrier *Lafayette*, the cruiser *Newfoundland* and the destroyers *Consort, Concord, Cockade, Cossack* and *Tobruk*. The exercises were marred by a tragic collision on Wednesday 28 March when, during a mock attack on Hong Kong Harbour, two of *Centaur's* Sea Hawks crashed near a rocky peak overlooking the eastern entrance of the harbour. Both the pilots were killed and a local Chinese woman died from burns after the engine and a fuel tank from one aircraft fell on her house. Wreckage also fell on a nearby school which, fortunately, was unoccupied at the time.

The exercise was followed by 'Operation Monsoon' involving a mock battle in the South China Sea, in which vital tanker convoys between Singapore, Manila and Hong Kong had to be protected from submarine attack. During the afternoon of Wednesday 4 April, with the exercises completed, the *Albion* entered Hong Kong Harbour and tied up alongside the North Arm of the Naval Dockyard. This time the visit lasted 12 days, which must have boosted the takings in the China Fleet Club and in the more dubious bars of Wanchai. On board the *Albion* receptions were held for the Governor of the Colony and for Sir Robert Scott, Britain's Special Commissioner for South-East Asia.

At 7.30am on Monday 16 April 1956 the *Albion's* visit to Hong Kong came to an end when she and the *Centaur* left the 'fragrant harbour' bound, once again, for Singapore. This time the two-day stop-over in the island colony was quite definitely a 'flag showing' occasion, for both the *Albion* and *Centaur* anchored in Singapore's Inner Roads, off Clifford Pier, in the heart of the city. Several VIPs were entertained on board and after dark the two ships' port sides were floodlit. Both *Albion* and *Centaur* left Singapore on Saturday 21 April and set courses west for the Red Sea. The *Albion's* first 'Crossing the Line' ceremony was held on 26 April in the Indian Ocean and on Wednesday 2 May she anchored in Suez Bay ready for her northbound transit of the Canal which took place the next day.

During a 24-hour call at Grand Harbour, FOAC Rear-Admiral Pedder struck his flag and went ashore, and then the *Albion* proceeded to Gibraltar for a 48-hour visit. Returning to the UK, she arrived off Falmouth on Monday 14 May and the squadrons were flown off to Culdrose and Lossiemouth. Early the next morning *Albion* anchored in the Spithead Roads to await Customs clearance, and at

5pm the same day she went alongside Pitch House Jetty, Portsmouth Dockyard, at the end of her first commission which had begun on the Tyne two years earlier. During that time the *Albion* had steamed 81,527 miles and had used 65,742 tons of FFO. It is also interesting to note that 600 tons of potatoes, 15,968 pounds of tea and 59,270 pints of rum had been consumed by the ship's company, although not necessarily in that order!

On Tuesday 19 June 1956 Captain Hawkins bade farewell to the *Albion*, which was now in the capable hands of Portsmouth Dockyard. Six days later President Nasser of Egypt announced that he intended to nationalize the Suez Canal, and so the stage was set for the *Albion's* next commission.

At 9.35am on Saturday 15 September 1956, *Albion* left her berth at Portsmouth's Middle Slip Jetty and, with full ceremony, put to sea bound for the Mediterranean and 'Operation Musketeer'.

Chapter Five

The Second Commission - 'Operation Musketeer'

British troops had first gone to Egypt in 1882 in order to suppress a military uprising against the Turkish Sultan, the Khedive and, contrary to the original intentions, they had remained there. During the Second World War this military presence had reached enormous proportions, with hundreds of thousands of British troops based in the country. However, the presence of these forces in what was an independent country had provoked nationalist violence in the form of riots and the killing of British servicemen. In 1945 Egypt's Prime Minister, Nokrashy Pasha, who was negotiating the revision of the 1936 Treaty with Britain, summed up the problem from the Egyptian point of view. He declared that, 'The presence of foreign troops on our soil, even if stationed in a distant area, is wounding to the national dignity.' In July 1952 King Farouk was deposed by a junta of fiercely nationalistic army officers, including Colonel Gamel Abdel Nasser who had led a nationalist movement amongst Egyptian army officers during the Second World War, and consequently had been detained by the British Military authorities in Egypt. The junta's nominee, Major-General Mohammed Neguib, who was now Prime Minister, lost no time in starting negotiations for the evacuation of the British forces from the Suez Canal Zone, with Colonel Nasser heading the Egyptian delegation. However, in April 1954 Nasser became Prime Minister and Neguib was relegated to a 'puppet' role as President. In October that year an agreement was reached whereby British troops would be withdrawn over a period of 20 months while the depot areas at Ismailia and Fayid would continue to be manned by 1,200 British civilians, for there were clauses in the agreement which provided for a British reoccupation in the event of an attack against Egypt by an outside power. The agreement was the best which Britain could hope for and by that time, with Egyptian nationalists fomenting violence within local populations, the British forces had become virtual prisoners within the base areas with internal security taking up most of their time and resources. Given this factor, together with the enormous expense of maintaining the base area, it was clearly unrealistic to suppose that British troops could continue to be stationed in Egypt in the post-war times. Added to this was the fact that the Suez Canal Company's concession was due for renewal in 1968 and it was quite clear that Nasser would never agree to that, which meant that the Suez Canal itself would have to be handed over to the Egyptian government.

Albion alongside Gibraltar's South Mole. *(FAAM)*

Before operations against Egypt started, and between flying exercises, *Albion* made a number of visits to Grand Harbour. In this view she lies at No 6 buoy in a very picturesque setting with a troopship in the background.

(FAAM)

During 1955 political relations between Britain and Egypt continued to deteriorate, particularly over the British government's treaty with Turkey and Iraq, which became known as the Baghdad Pact as it was signed in that city, and to which Nasser was opposed. In March 1956 the main body of British troops left the Canal Zone and on 13 June 1956, three days before the date which had been agreed, the last British troops left Egypt when the rearguard handed over Navy House to the Governor of Port Said, and then left by sea. Eleven days later Colonel Nasser replaced Neguib as President when he promulgated a new constitution which gave him sweeping powers.

Political events moved quickly after that and on 20 July 1956 Britain and America withdrew their offer of financial aid to Egypt to assist with the building of the Aswan Dam. There were two basic reasons for this; the first was the feeling that Egypt was stringing the West along while courting a better offer from the Soviet Union, and secondly there were serious doubts about Egypt's ability to repay any such loan. It seems that Nasser was not surprised by the decision of the western powers, but on 22 July the announcement by the Soviet Foreign Minister that no such assistance had been offered by the Eastern Bloc was, it seems, quite unexpected. For President Nasser this left only one other source of revenue - the Suez Canal, and on 26 July 1956 he announced its immediate nationalization. The next day, in London, the Prime Minister, Sir Anthony Eden, instructed the Chiefs of Staff to prepare plans for the reoccupation of the Suez Canal Zone, just over six weeks after the last British troops had left Egypt. Unfortunately, from the very start the political thinking was confused. Was the idea simply to topple Nasser or was it to 'internationalize' the Suez Canal? What were the long-term

aims of a military occupation and how would the problem of terrorism which had dogged the Suez Canal base prior to the withdrawal be overcome? These were just some of the questions which divided public opinion right from the start.

Meanwhile, as these momentous political events were played out on the world stage, the *Albion* was moored at Pitch House Jetty, Portsmouth, undergoing a refit which was scheduled for completion in October that year, when she would undergo her trials and work-up. Captain R. M. Smeeton MBE RN had been appointed as her commanding officer and on 25 July the new ship's company got to know each other, helped by an athletics meeting and a swimming gala at Pitt Street in the city. The recommissioning ceremony was held the next day, 26 July 1956, and work then continued on the refit. However, on 30 July the Admiralty called for an urgent report on the earliest date by which the refit and work-up could be completed, and at a conference it was decided that this would be 8 September, so a target date of 15 September was set for the embarkation of the squadrons. This was a month earlier than had been originally planned and everyone turned-to with a will, with the ship's company working until 6pm or 7pm each evening and the dockyard staff working round the clock on a shift system. Throughout August storing and hull and machinery maintenance continued unabated, with the pace of work getting faster as the deadline approached. However, there was a little time for relaxation and on Sunday 2 September there was a 'Families Day', when the *Albion* was opened to invited guests but on the following three days ammunitioning ship proceeded in earnest.

After a lot of hard work from everyone *Albion* was, in fact, ready for sea on Friday 7 September 1956, but severe

The 'Three Musketeers' together for 'Operation Musketeer'. *Eagle, Albion* (centre) and *Bulwark* exercising together in the Mediterranean. *(FAAM)*

gales prevented any movement in the harbour and she finally sailed at 3.15pm on Saturday 8 September for a six-day shakedown period prior to leaving the UK for the Mediterranean. That same afternoon a full power trial was conducted before the ship anchored in St Helens Roads off the Isle of Wight. The next day DF calibrations were carried out at the anchorage and when this was completed the remainder of the day was declared a rest period, in consideration of the great effort all had put in. During the afternoon a number of sporting activities were pursued, with Captain Smeeton's 'Elderly Officers Brigade' winning a deck hockey knock-out competition - all the other teams having been exhausted by earlier rounds.

At 6am on Monday 10 September *Albion* weighed anchor for flying trials which went on well into the evening before she anchored for the night in Sandown Bay. These trials were resumed the next day and they were finally completed at 7.15pm, when the trials party was disembarked in St Helens Roads. Wednesday 12 September started early for the *Albion* when she got under way at 3am and steamed to Portland where she fuelled from RFA *Tidereach*. By midday she had completed her DG ranging trials. However, the same day a signal was received from C-in-C Portsmouth, in response to Captain Smeeton's reports of machinery

defects which had developed, to the effect that the ship should endeavour to make Portsmouth that evening for the necessary work to be put in hand. As a result of this a towing exercise was abandoned and at 6.50pm the carrier secured alongside Pitch House Jetty.

Although the ship remained at eight hours' notice for steam, leave was granted to the ship's company. Then at 9.35am on Saturday 15 September HMS *Albion* slipped from her berth and with full ceremony, and the band playing in the open for the first time, she put to sea. As she steamed past Southsea Common a Swordfish flew low over the ship in salute, a gesture which Captain Smeeton took to be a good omen. That afternoon, as the ship steamed in the Channel, south of the Isle of Wight, *Albion* embarked 19 Sea Hawks of 800 and 802 Squadrons, eight Sea Venoms of 809 Squadron and four Skyraiders of 849 C Flight, before courses were set for Ushant and Gibraltar.

Before she left home waters two signals were received on board, both of which reflected the hard work which had been put in by the ship's company. The first, from the First Sea Lord, read, 'Congratulations on the speed and manner in which *Albion* has been prepared for further service.' The second was from the C-in-C Home Fleet: 'I know that in preparing your fine ship for service, officers and men have

A Sea Venom returns to *Albion* after a sortie over Egypt. *(FAAM)*

Sea Hawks parked forward during a lull in operations. *(FAAM)*

had to postpone leave and work long hours. I am happy that all demands have been met with great cheerfulness and a fine spirit. *Albion* has made a fine start to her commission. I wish all on board good luck, success in your forthcoming duties, and a happy return.'

The passage south was uneventful, with the weather fine, and on Monday 17 September *Albion* arrived off Gibraltar. Here flying exercises began in earnest with RAF North Front in the colony providing a diversion airfield. The area chosen for flying off Gibraltar was to the south of Punta Almina and, apart from thick fog off the North African coast, it proved ideal and remarkably free of shipping. During the voyage to Gibraltar two very serious leaks in main steam lines had developed and on 20 September the vessel docked alongside Gibraltar's South Mole in order that repairs could be carried out. During the three-day stay the ship's company took on, and defeated, the garrison teams at

soccer and hockey, and the water polo team trounced the Army team 6-0. Before leaving Gibraltar on Sunday 23 September Ceremonial Divisions were inspected and marched past. Shortly after leaving the port a request for medical assistance was received from RFA *Echodale*, which was some 200 miles east of Gibraltar. *Albion* steamed to intercept her and when the ships were 75 miles apart a Whirlwind helicopter carrying Surgeon Lieutenant D. J. Cripps RN was dispatched and he was winched onto the RFA, where he diagnosed an acute case of laryngitis.

On the morning of 25 September the *Albion* arrived in the waters off Cyprus, and on the following day she rendezvoused with HMS *Eagle*, wearing the flag of FOAC, Vice-Admiral M. L. Power CB CBE DSO, who transferred to *Albion* by helicopter to address the ship's company. Egypt and the Suez Canal was on everyone's mind at that time although, as Mr Syd Elmes, who was in *Albion* recalls,

Arming bombs during 'Operation Musketeer'.

Not many spare parking lots. A hangar scene during operations against Egypt.
(FAAM)

'As the political negotiations were in full swing it did not seem that the problem would involve the *Albion*.'

The last three days of September 1956 were spent in Malta and at 9am on 1 October she left the port to rendezvous with both *Eagle* and *Bulwark* for some very intensive flying exercises in the area. On Wednesday 10 October the *Albion's* aircraft took part in a large combined RAF/RN fly-past over Valletta, and two days later they clocked up their 1,000th arrested deck landing since leaving Portsmouth. After an 11-day break in Grand Harbour, on 23 October *Albion* was at sea once again with the ship at flying stations from 8am until midnight. During the evening of 24 October a Sea Hawk was lost when it ditched on take-off, but fortunately the pilot was picked up unhurt by the seaboat.

On Friday 26 October the three carriers returned to Grand Harbour and they sailed again on the morning of Monday 29 October 1956, just eight hours before the Israeli assault on Egyptian forces in the Sinai began. This time the vessels were bound for the Cyprus area and at 6pm all the ships were darkened and 'action stations' was exercised. Syd Elmes recalls that on board *Albion* the ship's company were issued with inflatable life-jackets and even personal weapons. He received a Lanchester sub-machine-gun, which he duly cleaned and oiled as instructed, and then returned it to the armoury, never to see it again. He remembers the morning of Tuesday 30 October vividly: 'I finished my watch in the tiller flat and went up on deck for a breath of fresh air. Imagine my surprise when, as far as I could see on all sides of the ship, there were vessels of all types and sizes - warships, tankers and transports. It was a fantastic sight and I guess that there must have been a lot of French ships involved as well. Later that day an announcement was made over the tannoy which informed us that Israeli forces had invaded Egypt and about 36 hours later we were told that we too were involved in the hostilities, and the first of our air sorties began.'

The joint British and French invasion of Egypt, code-named 'Operation Musketeer', had as its objective the securing of the Suez Canal, and in order to protect the landings a very heavy effort by the carrier strike-force, *Eagle*, *Albion* and *Bulwark* was required. Firstly it was imperative to destroy the Egyptian Air Force which was the largest in the Middle East, having been equipped with Soviet MiGs and Ilyushins. It also possessed some of the finest air bases which, ironically, had formerly been RAF airfields. The largest of these bases, Abu Sueir, ten miles west of Ismailia, had only been evacuated by the RAF on 10 March that year and just three weeks later the first MiGs moved in. However, as the aircraft had only recently been acquired by the Egyptians, their effectiveness was very much an unknown quantity.

Late in the evening of 31 October the British carriers ('The Three Musketeers'), together with their screening ships, arrived in the operational area 'Alfa', which was a circle of 35 miles' radius with its centre at a position Lat 32° - 40'N/Long 31° - 20'E, about 95 miles from Port Said. At 2.40am on Thursday 1 November 1956, 36 hours after a British/French ultimatum to both Egypt and Israel to withdraw their military forces ten miles from the Suez Canal within 12 hours had been ignored by Egypt, the flying operations from the British carriers commenced, when a Skyraider was launched on a reconnaissance flight. Two hours later a CAP mission was launched and then, at 5.20am, the dawn strikes were launched against airfield targets. Subsequently, strikes, CAP missions and AEW patrols were flown throughout each day, together with photo-reconnaissance and transport sorties, with the last aircraft being recovered at about 6.30pm every evening. This pattern continued for six days and, as the likelihood of attack by Egyptian aircraft decreased, CAP missions were reduced and the three carriers moved to within 60 miles of Port Said.

Apart from the fact that the three British carriers were bedevilled by catapult failures[*], the operations by all the Fleet Air Arm Squadrons were a complete success and *Albion's* aircraft made 415 sorties in six days. (*Albion* was withdrawn for replenishment on 3 November.) A measure of that success, particularly against the air bases, was the fact that the Allied invasion force landed on the beaches at Port Said on Monday 5 November 1956, with very little opposition.

On board the *Albion*, and among the rest of the fleet, morale was high as Syd Elmes recalls: 'We were kept informed of all the air strikes and the actions which involved the other ships. We were given a blow-by-blow account of the strikes carried out by *Albion's* squadrons against troop movements, military targets and communications networks.

They also carried out many raids against armoured vehicles in the desert.' In addition to the sorties made by the *Albion's* fixed-wing squadrons, her two Whirlwind helicopters made 130 sorties which included plane-guard duties and the evacuation of casualties.

However, despite the successful landings and the fact that, by the evening of 6 November, British and French ground forces were advancing rapidly towards Ismailia, the political realities were such that a cease-fire was ordered for midnight that night and it was agreed that all British and French forces would be 'withdrawn forthwith' and that they would be replaced by a United Nations force.

The *Albion* spent the remainder of November in the waters of the Levant, off Port Said, providing CAP patrols to cover the massive withdrawal operation code-named 'Operation Harridon'. On 12 November she received a visit from FOAC and five days later Lt-General Sir Hugh Stockwell, the Commander of the Land Forces, visited the ship. At 7.10pm on Monday 26 November 1956 the *Albion* was detached from the carrier group and ordered to proceed to Malta where she was to replenish her stores. She arrived in Grand Harbour on the morning of 29 November and the following day she went alongside Parlatorio Wharf. Syd Elmes recalls the return: 'Following the cease-fire we remained on station until late November, when we returned to Malta. During the campaign our mail had been heavily censored, and with the added restriction of being closed up at action stations for long periods, we were very much out of touch with political events. On our arrival in Malta, therefore, it came as a great surprise to hear what was being said at home about the campaign, and all the opposition to it - we had no inkling about any of that and, speaking personally, my conscience was clear as I had done my duty without hesitation.'

During her stay at Malta Ceremonial Divisions were held and Admiral Sir Guy Grantham GCB CBE DSO, C-in-C Mediterranean, visited Captain Smeeton. Then on 11 December 1956, 24 hours after the *Bulwark*, the *Albion* left harbour once again bound for the waters of the Levant. Two days later the First Lord of the Admiralty, Viscount Hailsham, visited the ship and addressed the ship's company. On Sunday 23 December 1956, with the British and French withdrawal from Port Said complete, *Albion* sailed for Grand Harbour where she arrived early on Christmas Day.

'Operation Musketeer' was over, but the political repercussions would reverberate for at least 20 years afterwards. There followed a thorough streamlining of all the Armed Forces and the course was set for *Albion's* future career, for the value of a helicopter assault from an aircraft-carrier which could carry up to 1,000 Royal Marines had been demonstrated.

---

[*] *Eagle's* starboard catapult was unserviceable throughout the operation; for most of the morning of 6 November both *Bulwark's* catapults were unserviceable and during most of 4 November *Albion* could use only one catapult.

Chapter Six

The Second Commission And Royal Occasions

After their mammoth effort of the previous five months, *Albion's* ship's company were able to enjoy their 1956 Christmas Dinner and the New Year at Malta. On Boxing Day there was a concert in the hangar, the stars of the show being the Wrens' choir from Whitehall Mansions. On 27 December work started on painting the ship for her first 'foreign' visit of the commission to Messina in Sicily. Although the port is not very large, the *Albion* was able to go alongside and during the four days in harbour large crowds of locals queued to get on board when the ship was open to visitors, whilst the ship's company were able to go on coach tours to Taormina and snow-capped Mount Etna. Neville Clements, who was a Leading Airman at the time, recalls that when *Albion* left the port at 3pm on Monday 14 January, there were still long queues of people waiting to go on board. He remembers at one stage, the situation becoming rather tense, with the duty watch being called out to man hoses and, if necessary, 'repel boarders'. Three days later *Albion* was back in Grand Harbour and alongside Parlatorio Wharf in French Creek, very close to the Fleet Canteen, where she remained for six days. Shortly before entering harbour the Sea Hawks were flown off to Hal Far and during the stay in Malta personnel of 824 (Gannets) and 845 (Whirlwind helicopters) Squadrons were embarked. Thus loaded *Albion* left Malta on Tuesday 22 January,

bound for Marseilles where she was to make a five-day courtesy call.

Once at sea the Gannets and anti-submarine Whirlwinds were embarked and flying exercises continued during the voyage to the southern French port. Unfortunately, the visit was sadly marred by the deaths of three petty officers who were drowned when a dinghy they were sailing was overturned when a sudden, very severe, squall blew up. Despite extensive searches by the ship's helicopters and the seaboat, only one body was recovered, that of Petty Officer Simmons. The funeral service was held at the British Military Cemetery and Captain Smeeton, together with a good number of the ship's company, were in attendance. Next morning, at 9.30am on Wednesday 30 January 1957, *Albion* left Marseilles for Gibraltar, the loss of three members of the ship's company having cast a shadow over the visit. There then followed a month of exercises with ships of the Home Fleet and the US Sixth Fleet, including the carriers *Ark Royal*, USS *Lake Champlain* and USS *Forrestal*. The first exercise, 'Buckshot', also included the submarines *Walrus* and *Andrew* and on its completion on Friday 7 February, *Albion* went alongside Gibraltar's South Mole. The following morning FOAC hoisted his flag in *Albion* and the Royal Yacht arrived with HRH The Duke of Edinburgh on board, who expressed a wish to go to sea with the *Albion*. He

1956 Christmas celebrations were held in Malta - but only just. *(FAAM)*

On 7 February 1957 HRH The Duke of Edinburgh spent a day on board watching flying exercises. Here, escorted by Captain Smeeton, he is about to return to the Royal Yacht.
(FAAM)

embarked at 7.20am the next morning and 15 minutes later *Albion* slipped her moorings and put to sea. After watching the flying exercises that morning and making a tour of the ship, he transferred back to the Royal Yacht, this time by jackstay. During the exercises which took place the following week, the C-in-C Home Fleet, Admiral Sir John Eccles KCB KCVO CBE, hoisted his flag in *Albion* for three days. Then on 27 February, with the exercises completed, the Gannets and Whirlwinds of 825 and 845 Squadrons flew off to RAF North Front and *Albion* returned to Gibraltar's South Mole. The following day she embarked the personnel of 800 and 802 Squadrons, the intention being that when she returned to sea the Sea Hawks, which had remained at Malta, would

return. Unfortunately no one had reckoned on the Portuguese Navy.

On Friday 1 March *Albion* was still alongside at Gibraltar and during the day a number of VIPs visited the ship. In the afternoon FOAC Admiral Power was, fortunately, ashore. At 3pm the *Nuno Tristao*, the first of four visiting Portuguese frigates, entered harbour and after exchanging salutes she was berthed aft of the *Albion*. At 3.20pm she was followed by a second frigate, the *Diego Gomez* which, whilst manoeuvring to her berth alongside the first vessel, hit the *Albion's* stern with her stem. The force of the collision tore a large hole in the Admiral's Day Cabin on the starboard side. Fortunately there were no injuries and Admiral Power's comments to the Portuguese C-in-C, Admiral De Drion, whom he met the next day, are not recorded.

The damage to *Albion* could not be repaired at Gibraltar and so the next day, after tarpaulins had been rigged to cover the carrier's damaged stern, *Albion* left for Portsmouth. During the voyage north speed was adjusted in order that the covers remained secure and not too much water found its way inboard. The *Albion* was the last of the three carriers to have taken part in 'Operation Musketeer', and there was great interest in her return home. When she was off the Lizard, HRH The Duke of Gloucester, accompanied by Press reporters, embarked by helicopter for the overnight passage to Spithead. At 6.15am on Wednesday 6 March *Albion* anchored at Spithead to await Customs clearance and later that morning the Duke of Gloucester and Admiral Power left the ship by helicopter. At 2.15pm *Albion* was under way once again and at just before 3pm she was safely secured alongside South Railway Jetty where families of the ship's company, who had been waiting patiently for most of the day, were able to go on board to greet their loved ones. The ship had been away for five months, during which time she had spearheaded the air offensive against Egyptian forces, but the only damage she had suffered during that time had been inflicted by our oldest ally.

During her six-week stay in Portsmouth leave was taken by the ship's company and the damage to the carrier's stern was repaired. On Tuesday 16 April *Albion* slipped her berth and sailed once again for the Mediterranean. She steamed to Malta without calling at Gibraltar and during the week-long voyage flying exercises took place on most days, with the Sea Hawks of 800 and 802 Squadrons having finally re-embarked. Although she arrived off Malta on Tuesday 23 April, it was another two days before she entered Grand Harbour and berthed alongside Parlatorio Wharf. During her ten-day stay in Malta she was visited by the C-in-C Mediterranean Fleet, Admiral Sir Ralph A. B. Edwards KCB CBE, and on Sunday 4 May she left to rendezvous with the French aircraft-carrier *Bois Belleau**, for 'Exercise

* Ex-USS *Belleau Wood*, an Independence-class carrier which had taken an active part in the Pacific War and which, in October 1944, had been severely damaged by kamikaze aircraft off Leyte.

HRH The Duke of Edinburgh is transferred by jackstay from *Albion* to the Royal Yacht. *(FAAM)*

The damage caused to *Albion's* stern by the Portuguese frigate *Diego Gomez.*

(FAAM)

Medflex Epic' for which *Albion* again operated in an anti-submarine role. This lasted for nine days and on completion *Albion* set course for Gibraltar and Rosyth, stopping only briefly at Gibraltar and for three hours at Spithead in order to obtain Customs clearance. At 7.30am on Friday 17 May 1957 *Albion* moored off Rosyth in readiness for a thorough sprucing up before taking part in 'Operation Steadfast'.

This was to be a review of ships of the Home Fleet in the Cromarty Firth by Her Majesty The Queen. The review was to take place between Monday 27 and Wednesday 29 May and during this time the Queen and the Duke of Edinburgh were scheduled to visit the *Albion* twice. During the three days spent at Rosyth the ship's company practised Queen's Divisions, and following the *Albion's* arrival in the Cromarty Firth on Wednesday 22 May, there was a rehearsal of the review itself with the

Maidstone assuming the role of the Royal Yacht. As the ship's company practised Divisions there was a constant stream of theatrically dressed parties embarking and disappearing into the hangar to rehearse for the concert which was to be held on board.

On Saturday 25 May FOAC raised his flag in *Albion* and at 7.30am on Monday 27 May the ship put to sea to rendezvous with the Royal Yacht and the other ships in the review, 20 in all including the *Eagle* and *Ark Royal.* After firing a royal 21-gun salute the fleet steamed past the *Britannia.* On completion of the review the fleet formed up to follow *Britannia* through the Moray Firth and the mile and a half-wide mouth of the Cromarty Firth, between the twin 600ft-high 'Sutors of Cromarty' to the anchorage at Invergordon. That afternoon schools in Easter Ross and the Black Isle were closed early so that the children could go down and watch their arrival. By 5.30pm

The damaged stem of the offender and... *(FAAM)*

...Shipwrights examine the new ventilation facility in the Admiral's Day Cabin. *(FAAM)*

the whole fleet was at anchor and that evening all the ships were illuminated, which provided a magnificent sight.

Next morning at 10am *Albion's* ship's company fell in on the flight deck for Divisions, together with men from the destroyers *Alamein* and *Barrosa*. Just over half an hour later Her Majesty The Queen and HRH The Duke of Edinburgh, accompanied by Vice-Admiral Power and Captain Smeeton, inspected the assembled Divisions before leaving for other ships of the fleet. At 8.45pm that evening the Queen, Duke of Edinburgh and the C-in-C Home Fleet, Admiral Sir John Eccles KCB KCVO CBE, returned on board to watch a fleet concert in C hangar. At 9am on the morning of Wednesday 29 May the ships' companies of the assembled fleet mustered to salute the *Britannia* as she left Invergordon at the conclusion of the review and later that morning the fleet dispersed. *Albion* steamed south

from Invergordon and during the voyage to Portsmouth the squadrons were kept busy with night-flying exercises. After a short period in Portsmouth Dockyard the *Albion*, wearing the flag of FOAC, was at sea again, this time accompanied by the *Maidstone* and bound for Oslo by way of the Straits of Dover and the North Sea. The two ships went alongside in the Norwegian capital on the afternoon of Monday 24 June and the highlight of the week-long visit was the ship's company dance which was held in C hangar on the second evening.

On leaving Olso the *Albion* got back to work again with flying exercises, this time closely observed by a Soviet Sverdlov-class cruiser. During the following week, after two very wet and windy Navy Days at Rosyth, came the Admiral's inspection, while the *Albion* lay at a Spithead anchorage. On Thursday 11 July 1957 Vice-Admiral Power,

Albion leads *Ark Royal* into the Cromarty Firth for 'Operation Steadfast', the Royal Review of the Home Fleet in May 1957. *(FAAM)*

Monday 27 May 1957 and *Albion*, with hands fallen in to port, steams past the Royal Yacht. Astern of the *Britannia* is HMS *Apollo*, flying the flag of the C-in-C Home Fleet. *(FAAM)*

An aerial view of *Albion* as she steams past
Britannia.   *(FAAM)*

A view taken from the *Eagle* during the steam-past
showing the *Albion* and astern of her, the *Ark Royal.*
(FAAM)

An aerial view of the steam-past with the
Albion in the centre.   *(FAAM)*

During the morning of Tuesday 28 May 1957 Her Majesty The Queen inspected Divisions on board *Albion*. Also present were ratings from HM Ships *Alamein*, *Reward*, and *Barrosa*. HMS *Eagle* is in the background. *(FAAM)*

Her Majesty The Queen, accompanied by HRH The Duke of Edinburgh, escorted by Vice-Admiral M. L. Power, FOAC, and Captain Smeeton, leaves the flight deck. *(FAAM)*

FOAC, inspected the carrier from truck to keel and from stem to stern, after which Ceremonial Divisions were held. The FOAC was well satisfied and it is worth quoting his official report: 'HMS *Albion* was commissioned and rushed out of refit in record time. She has been kept very hard at it ever since. She acquitted herself bravely in "Operation Musketeer" and has continued to do so in every circumstance within my knowledge. The ship is well commanded, well led, happy, versatile and very enterprising. I am thoroughly satisfied with her.'

After a short stay in Portsmouth, *Albion* put to sea again on the afternoon of Monday 15 July, in company with *Ark Royal*. Over the next eleven days the two carriers gave daily demonstrations of naval air power to MPs, the Press, officers of the Staff College and, last but not least, to groups of Wrens. These manoeuvres earned the praises of

both the C-in-C Home Fleet and the C-in-C Portsmouth and they were broken only by a 48-hour call at Dover during the weekend of 20/21 July.

Following the summer leave period at Portsmouth, which included two much sunnier Navy Days, *Albion* left her home port for the final leg of her second commission and participation in the largest NATO exercise ever held, 'Exercise Strikeback'. Up to 100 ships took part in the ten-day exercise in the North Atlantic. At the conclusion of the exercise, on Sunday 29 September, *Albion* anchored for the day in Belfast Lough and that afternoon her sister ship *Bulwark*, also returning from 'Strikeback', passed by as she made her way to Belfast for a courtesy visit. The *Albion*, however, was soon bound for Portsmouth and seven days alongside South Railway Jetty.

Albion's final deployment of the commission got under

way at 1pm on Friday 11 October when, wearing the flag of the newly appointed FOAC, Rear-Admiral H. C. D. McLean DSC, she left Portsmouth bound for Gibraltar and exercises with both *Eagle* and *Ark Royal*. Her final foreign visit, with the *Ark Royal*, was a four-day call at Lisbon on Tuesday 22 October, when both ships anchored in the River Tagus beside the city. During the visit a children's party was held on board for youngsters of the sizeable British community, but even the warm sunny weather of Lisbon could not distract the thoughts of the ship's company from returning to Portsmouth - and home.

Albion left the Tagus on Saturday 26 October and the following day FOAC transferred his flag to the *Ark Royal*.

Two days later *Albion* was secure alongside Portsmouth's Middle Slip Jetty for the last time in her second commission. On 4 November 1957 she provided overnight accommodation for Captain P. D. Gick OBE DSC RN and 100 officers and ratings from *Bulwark*, which was undergoing a ten-day self-maintenance period, and when they had disembarked the de-ammunitioning and destoring of the *Albion* began. On Monday 18 November 1957 Captain Smeeton relinquished command and *Albion* was taken into dockyard hands for a seven-month refit. It had been a very eventful 14 months since she had been recommissioned in such a hurry in September 1956.

During the evening of Tuesday 28 May 1957 a Fleet Concert was held in the *Albion's* hangar. In this view Captain Smeeton escorts Her Majesty to her seat. *(FAAM)*

Chapter Seven

The Third Commission - World Cruise 1958-59

On Thursday 10 May 1958 Captain A. B. Cole DSC RN was appointed to command the *Albion*, which was nearing the end of her refit at 5B3 berth in Portsmouth Dockyard's No 3 Basin. Ten days later 300 members of the ship's company gathered together in the gymnasium of Pompey Barracks and marched down to the ship to join the intrepid bunch who were 'hanging over' from the previous commission. No sooner had the last man stepped on board, when the dockyard decided to move *Albion* to Pitch House Jetty. The next day saw the Commissioning Service, which was conducted in the hangar by the Chaplain of the Fleet and attended by a good many families.

Throughout the following weeks the ship began to take on some semblance of order and during the afternoon of Thursday 19 June 1958 *Albion* left Portsmouth for her sea trials, after seven months in dockyard hands. After landing on the squadrons the ship steamed north to Scottish waters where the flying trials were to take place. On the morning of Tuesday 15 July she was off Rathlin Island when news broke that a group of Iraqi army officers, led by a Brigadier Kassim, had assassinated King Feisel, his son and the country's Prime Minister, and proclaimed a republic. Although King Hussein of Jordan and the Lebanese government appealed to the US and Britain for help, it did not appear that *Albion* would become involved and she continued her voyage north. However, on Thursday 17 July, when she was in the Cromarty Firth, she received a

signal ordering her to return 'with all dispatch' to Portsmouth. All next day she steamed south and passed Dover in the early hours of Saturday 19 July. That morning her squadrons were flown off and during the afternoon she was berthed in C Lock at Portsmouth Dockyard.

There then followed three hectic days as *Albion* was virtually transformed into a commando carrier so that she could carry the whole of 42 Commando RM and 361 officers and men of the 19th Infantry Brigade Group, together with nearly 500 vehicles, to Malta to reinforce the Army in the Middle East. It had been decided to send two battalions of troops to Amman in order to bolster up King Hussein's government. Dockyard technicians welded more than 1,000 eye bolts to *Albion's* flight deck and to one of the hangars, the rest of the hangar space being converted into an enormous dormitory, with a veritable forest of tubular steel frames and canvas bunks. Teams of seamen worked in relays round the clock to complete the task and, as a finishing touch, each bunk was provided with a paper bag, 'seasick, for the use of'. As always *Albion's* tremendous team spirit came to the fore and at 9.45pm on Saturday 19 July the loading of the army trucks was started and less than 24 hours later the troops began to embark. Finally, after a herculean effort by everyone concerned, at 4.15pm on Tuesday 22 July, with army vehicles almost covering the flight deck and with troops lining the few remaining spaces, *Albion* left Portsmouth and set courses for Ushant and Gibraltar. During her passage to Malta she made only

A Scimitar practising 'touch and go' runs during *Albion's* work-up in June 1958.
(FAAM)

A Skyraider lands on during *Albion's* work up. *(FAAM)*

Starting up for flying exercises, June 1958. *(FAAM)*

A Sea Hawk breaks a wire on landing and almost slides overboard, June 1958. *(FAAM)*

Following a very hurried conversion *Albion* leaves Portsmouth on 22 July 1958 with Army reinforcements for the Middle East following the assassination of King Feisel of Iraq. It was almost a 'dry run' for her commando ship role. *(FAAM)*

a brief three-hour stop at Gibraltar for fuel and she arrived alongside Grand Harbour's Parlatorio Wharf at 6pm on Saturday 26 July. The whole operation, from the time of the receipt of the signal off the coast of Scotland to the time of unloading the last vehicle in Malta, took nine days.

On Monday 4 August, having cleared the flight deck of its eye bolts and the hangar of its bunks, and having embarked the maintenance personnel of 804 and 809 Squadrons and 849 C Flight, *Albion* put to sea in order to complete the flying trials and work-up which had been interrupted. There followed a short visit to Messina, where the ship's company were able to take advantage of a large European trade fair, complete with a Bavarian Bierhaus offering iced lager. The visit provided a welcome break in the ship's work-up programme, even though the football team lost 2-5 to an Italian Navy team.

After leaving Messina *Albion* took part in 'Exercise Casex 58' off Malta and rendezvoused with the *Eagle* for a voyage east to the Lebanon and Cyprus where they exercised with US warships. At the end of August, with political tensions in the Middle East easing, *Albion* was able to anchor off Famagusta where banyan and canteen leave

was granted, but only under armed guard, for Colonel George Grivas and his EOKA terrorists were very active at the time.

On Sunday 7 September *Albion* weighed anchor and left the beaches of Cyprus behind as she set course for Malta. Next day, whilst carrying out flying exercises, a Sea Hawk and a Sea Venom were involved in a mid-air collision just west of Cyprus. Fortunately all three crew members were rescued safely an hour later and *Albion* set courses for Gibraltar and then home. After flying off the squadrons in the Channel she arrived at Spithead early on the morning of 16 September, and that same evening she was secured in C Lock in Portsmouth Dockyard for work to be carried out on the starboard propeller and to prepare for her 'world cruise'. During her stay in Portsmouth long queues formed outside the Sick Bay as everyone received their yellow fever and cholera vaccinations. There was drama too when, at 12.45am on a beautiful moonlit autumn night, the quartermaster reported something 'large and black' come to the surface close to the ship. The ship's divers were roused and they carried out a search of the underwater hull and at dawn clearance divers from HMS *Vernon* were called upon

Only nine days after her recall from Scotland *Albion* arrives at Grand Harbour with reinforcements, on 26 July 1958. *(FAAM)*

Albion's flying trials, which had been interrupted by the Middle East crisis, were continued in the Mediterranean in August 1958. Here a Sea Hawk's oleo collapses on landing. *(FAAM)*

Alongside at Messina, August 1958. *(FAAM)*

After leaving Messina *Albion* took part in exercises off Cyprus with ships of the US Sixth Fleet. With the ship anchored off Famagusta banyan leave was granted but, with EOKA terrorists active, only under armed guard. Here, under the watchful eye of an alert sentry, *Albion's* ship's company enjoy the beaches of Cyprus. *(FAAM)*

to do the same, although there were rumours that it had been one of them who had been seen during the night. Eventually the Press blamed a porpoise for the excitement, but those 'in the know' still blamed *Vernon's* clearance divers.

Albion finally set off on her ten months' world trip on Monday 20 October 1958 and steamed directly to Malta. After only a five-hour stop at Gibraltar for fuel she arrived in Grand Harbour on Sunday 26 October, where she relieved the *Bulwark* which was returning to Portsmouth for conversion to a commando ship. After a 24-hour stop-over in Malta *Albion*, together with the cruiser *Sheffield* and the frigate *Chichester*, left for Port Said. On the way *Albion* rendezvoused and exercised with the *Eagle* and *Torquay*, arriving off Port Said in the early hours of Friday 31 October. It was the first time she had been through Suez since the Canal had been taken over by Nasser, and this time there were Russian-built destroyers and submarines moored outside Navy House, whilst overhead MiG17 fighter aircraft flew by. However, by 7pm the following day both *Albion* and *Chichester* had left Port Suez and entered the Red Sea. The two ships arrived in Aden on Wednesday 5 November to find the colony in the throes of a general strike, stirred up, no doubt, by Nasser's agents in the Yemen. However, this did not deter the Indian traders of Steamer Point from selling large numbers of shiny new cameras, each one accompanied by a suitably arranged receipt for eventual presentation to Customs. Fortunately the shark nets rigged up along the beaches at Tarshyne held firm, and on Monday 10 November *Albion* and *Chichester* left Aden for Karachi which was, in those days, the capital of Pakistan. Despite the fact that the city was under martial law, the five-day visit proved a success and most of the

Albion's mess-decks ended up with more than their fair share of Persian rugs and carpets.

After her call at Karachi *Albion* continued her long voyage east as she and *Chichester* set courses for Singapore. Off the northern coast of Sumatra they were met by the destroyer *Cavalier* and on the morning of Saturday 29 November the three ships arrived in the Naval Base where *Albion* was secured alongside No 8 berth in the dockyard. Two days later FO2 FES, Rear-Admiral V. C. Begg DSO, hoisted his flag in the *Albion* and would continue to do so for some five months. He later declared that this period of his service was, '...a great privilege and a pleasure to serve even for a relatively short time, in this happy and efficient ship.'

The ship's company had just two weeks in which to sample the well organized canteens and sports facilities of the Naval Base before, on Friday 12 December, they left for Hong Kong and the ever popular amenities which Wanchai had to offer. There were of course more formal occasions as well, and on 29 December HE The Governor was entertained on board by FO2 FES. As always Christmas and New Year in Hong Kong were a great success, but on Monday 5 January 1959 *Albion* left the colony for the antipodes. At 6.30am on Wednesday 14 January the ship crossed the Equator, and two and a half hours later saw the start of an extended 'Crossing the Line' routine. The fun started on the flight deck where, after some excellent planning by King Neptune and his court, Admiral Begg and Captain Cole were the first two to experience a double-ducking. Thereafter victims were rapidly dispatched in quick succession, including the volunteer band who had only turned out to greet FO2 FES.

Three days later *Albion* arrived at the remote outpost of Honiara, capital of the British Solomon Islands, which was

Monday 20 October 1958. *Albion* passes Southsea Common as she sails for the Far East. *(FAAM)*

Port Said, 31 October 1958. A southbound convoy forms up. *(FAAM)*

'Crossing the Line' *en route* to Auckland, 14 January 1959. *(FAAM)*

best known for the US Army's Second World War campaign at Guadalcanal. Unfortunately a steering defect caused a fixed-wing fly-past to be cancelled, and in the pouring rain it was doubtful whether the High Commissioner saw much of the 17-gun salute fired in his honour. Next day *Albion* battled through a cyclone as she steamed south once again, bound for Auckland. At just after midday on Thursday 22 January she anchored off Rangaunu Harbour in Great Exhibition Bay at the northern end of North Island in order to clean up some of the storm damage which she had suffered. One seaboat had been broken up and spread about the starboard boat deck, several sections of guard rail were missing and, worst of all for a flag-showing visit, all the fresh paintwork which had been carefully applied in Hong Kong by Jenny's Side Party, had peeled away to reveal layers of red rust and deposited salt. However, the seamen worked hard for ten hours to rectify the damage and then the ship was able to weigh anchor and proceed round the coast to Auckland, where she arrived alongside the Wynyard Wharf at 10.30am on Friday 23 January 1959.

The following day the *Albion* was opened to visitors and, despite the fact that it was a very hot day, queues started to form hours before the gangways were open. Although the local police did their best, they were obviously taken by surprise by the numbers that turned up. The local Press estimated the figure to be 15,000, and the ship's records show the number of visitors that day to be 14,960. The next day was a public holiday and the anniversary regatta enabled the *Albion's* boat crews to carry off a few prizes.

Following a happy four days in Auckland the *Albion* headed south for Wellington where Captain Cole gave a free demonstration of seamanship when, with the help of only one small tug, the carrier was berthed at Oatea Quay, Wellington, which was only ten feet longer than the ship herself. Admiral Begg, who had driven from Auckland, arrived back on board at 12.30pm that same day, which

Albion arrives alongside Wynyard Wharf, Auckland, on Friday 23 January 1959.
(FAAM)

gave him exactly 20 minutes to prepare before meeting the Prime Minister of New Zealand, Sir Walter Nash, and other dignitaries who were visiting the ship.

After a hectic four-day visit to Wellington *Albion* left New Zealand at 8.30am on Tuesday 3 February and set course across the Tasman Sea for Hobart. During the crossing the flight deck resounded to the tramp of marching feet as the ship's company rehearsed for a parade which was to be held in the streets of Hobart. Fortunately the order 'about-turn' was always given on time and nobody was lost overboard. On Friday 6 February, after a full ceremonial entry into the harbour, *Albion* tied up alongside Princes Wharf. The visit coincided with the island's Royal Regatta, which was usually attended by the Governor-General of Australia who, at that time, was Field Marshal Sir William Slim. Both he, and the city's Lord Mayor, Sir Archibald Park CMG, went on board the carrier and Sir Archibald, as an ex-RN leading stoker *circa* 1909, even hitched a lift to the next port of call, which was Sydney. Naturally he showed great interest in *Albion's* main machinery compartments and he was a popular visitor to the engine-rooms and boiler-rooms.

Albion arrived alongside Sydney's North End Wharf at just before 11am on Friday 13 February 1959 and, once again, the ship was thrown open to visitors. That evening, with the weather fine and warm, the official cocktail party could be held out in the open air on the flight deck. The 11-day visit to the city was, in fact, classed as a self-maintenance period but, unfortunately, it could not go on forever and at 8.30am on Tuesday 24 February the *Albion* left her berth in the city and set courses for Melbourne.

Two days later, at just after 4pm, whilst the ship was off

Jervis Bay, a Sea Venom crashed on take-off. Despite the fact that *Albion* went full astern, an extensive search failed to find any trace of the pilot, Lieutenant R. F. P. Carne RN, or the observer, Lieutenant D. I. Douglass RN. This tragic accident marred what would otherwise have been an enjoyable 48-hour visit to the small town of Jervis Bay *en route* to Melbourne. At 8.30am on Tuesday 3 March 1959 *Albion* docked alongside Princes Pier, Melbourne, and during the five-day stay the Australian 'Returned Services League' arranged a number of 'up country' visits for the ship's company.

Next came a six-day voyage across the Great Australian Bight during which planned flying exercises were cancelled owing to adverse weather conditions, but the *Albion* rejoined the *Chichester*, which had steamed down from Calcutta, and the destroyers HMAS *Voyager* and HMS *Cheviot*, together with the RFA *Resurgent*. All five ships then set course for Fremantle where they arrived on Saturday 14 March for a four-day visit.

With the antipodean cruise at an end, *Albion* and the other four ships steamed north, bound once again for Singapore. During the passage they were joined by HMAS *Melbourne* (originally intended as the light fleet carrier HMS *Majestic*, but never completed as such), and the cruisers HMNZS *Royalist* and HMS *Ceylon*. Apart from the exercises carried out by this sizeable fleet, the only real excitement came during the passage through the Sunda Strait when two Indonesian MiG17s flew low overhead to have a close look. However, on seeing the size of the naval force they retired hastily. Here too magnificent views of Mount Krakatoa by moonlight could be enjoyed. On the last day of March *Albion* was back alongside No 8 berth in

With the famous Harbour Bridge as a backdrop, *Albion* arrives at Sydney on Friday 13 February 1959. *(FAAM)*

Singapore Dockyard.

Before she left the Far East *Albion* took part in a large SEATO exercise, 'Sea Demon', which was sponsored by Australia and which involved the ships of five Navies; the US, British, Australian, New Zealand and French. In addition to the *Albion* two other carriers, the USS *Yorktown* and HMAS *Melbourne* were present. As well as the naval forces the exercise included shore-based fighters and bombers of the US Navy and RAF, operating from the Philippines and Singapore. For six days prior to the start of the exercises there were numerous 'conferences' at the Naval Base in Singapore, and there were some ugly rumours that one senior officer lost three quid at poker during one such 'conference'. *Albion* left Singapore on Monday 20 April and, in company with the *Melbourne* and *Yorktown*, set course for Manila. During the first phase of 'Sea Demon' *Albion* had the opportunity of cross operating with USS *Yorktown* and Trackers and Banshees from the American vessel soon became a familiar sight on *Albion's* flight deck. As a conclusion to the exercise aircraft from all three carriers flew past over the centre of Manila and its Capitol Building. During the exercise *Albion* had steamed 4,179 miles with her aircraft carrying out 516 sorties, and at 9am on Monday 4 May she returned to Singapore, where FO2 FES struck his flag. After an 18-day self-maintenance period, *Albion* and her faithful companion *Chichester* left Singapore for the last time during the commission, bound now for South Africa and South America. The previous day the C-in-C South Africa, South Atlantic, Admiral Sir R. Dymock-Watson KCB OBE, had hoisted his flag in *Albion*.

During the 11-day voyage across the Indian Ocean to her first port of call, Diego Suarez, Madagascar, a Sea Hawk was lost after ditching on take-off, but fortunately the pilot was rescued safely. At 8.40am on Tuesday 2 June 1959 the *Albion* reached her destination and anchored in the magnificent natural harbour of Diego Suarez, which was still littered with a number of wrecks dating back to the Second World War. From Madagascar *Albion* steamed south-west for the much more popular run ashore at Durban. Despite mist and rain enormous crowds gathered along the seafront and on jetties to welcome the carrier. Literally thousands of invitations from the local population were received on board, so many, in fact, that there were not enough members of the ship's company to go round. This hospitality was reciprocated when the ship was opened to private guests and there were almost as many visitors as on an open day. The six-day visit ended at 9am on Tuesday 16 June, when *Albion* left for Cape Town and her rendezvous with the *Chichester* which had been to Simonstown. However, as a parting gesture she was able to stage the fly-past which had been cancelled on arrival.

Three days after leaving Durban *Albion* tied up alongside her berth in Cape Town Harbour. Once again record crowds queued to visit the ship and on a hot, sunny afternoon a very successful open-air children's party was held on the flight deck. There were tears shed when, on the last day of June, *Albion* left Cape Town and set course west for South America and the final leg of the commission.

During visits to Buenos Aires and Rio de Janeiro it was proposed to give displays of naval aviation to senior government officials, and during the voyage across the South Atlantic Ocean the rehearsals were carried out for the first of these displays which would be held off the River Plate for Argentinian officials. *Albion* anchored off the breakwater at Montevideo at 11.55pm on Monday 13 July 1959, but the schedule did not then go according to plan. At 4.20am the next morning she got under way for the shallow water passage to Buenos Aires, but it seems that no one had foreseen the difficulties which could arise here, with the ship's engine-room intakes being situated directly underneath the hull. By 7.17am the condenser cooling water tubes were well and truly blocked with mud, as a result of which she lost vacuum in both engines and was left helpless, without any power at all. Captain Cole immediately dropped anchor and called for the assistance of tugs. Soon afterwards a very small specimen arrived, together with the Argentinian destroyer *Cervantes*, and both vessels milled around making helpful signals but were unable to do much else. Fortunately, when the tide rose the tug was able to manoeuvre *Albion* into the middle of the deep water channel where she could anchor again, but in so doing caused a massive obstruction for all the deep draught merchant shipping. Next day four tugs arrived and towed her further up the fairway towards the elusive Buenos Aires and at 6pm that day she anchored once more in the deep water channel.

All that day work went on as the engine-room staff laboured in shifts to remove tons of mud from the condenser tubes and at just after midnight on 16 July steam was raised and *Albion*, assisted by three tugs, set off for the open sea. At 4pm that afternoon she was back at the breakwater off Montevideo where she anchored in deep water. For the next 36 hours the engine-room staff worked flat out to clear the condenser tubes thoroughly, and finally, during the afternoon of Saturday 18 July, full power trials were successfully carried out as the ship steamed north to Rio de Janeiro where she arrived alongside during the afternoon of Thursday 23 July. Vice-Admiral Sir Patrick Symons KBE who was, at that time, a lieutenant with 809 Squadron and a newly trained AWF Observer, who had been drafted to *Albion* in Singapore to replace the late Lt D. I. Douglass, recalls the events: 'I was crewed up with the squadron's senior pilot, Lt-Cdr A. (Gus) Grey, and I experienced the hazards of night flying in a Sea Venom with one of the best pilots in the Navy. One notable event which I remember was *Albion* grounding in the River Plate *en route* to Buenos Aires, which we never reached. Captain

Open day for visitors at Melbourne on 4 March 1959. The Australian carrier *Melbourne* is berthed astern of *Albion*. *(FAAM)*

Albion enters Durban at 11.30am on Wednesday 10 June 1959. *(FAAM)*

During the 'Exercise Sea Demon' US Navy Banshees from the *Yorktown* cross-operated with the *Albion*. *(FAAM)*

Cole was widely reported as being most unhappy with the planned visit due to shifting sandbanks and the shallow waters of the delta. However, he was assured that all would be well in the hands of the local pilot and that it was highly desirable, for diplomatic reasons, that the visit should take place. Apparently no one recognized the problem which might be created by the main engine-room intakes which were on the bottom of the ship and, in consequence, mud was sucked into both main condensers and this resulted in a total engine failure. All hands worked in shifts to clean out the condensers and we were towed down channel by Argentinian tugs. Had it happened to me years later when in command of the *Bulwark* I would have been "mortified". However, as a junior aircrew spectator to the drama it was a great laugh, with a happy ending as we went straight to Rio de Janeiro and spent an extended and most enjoyable visit there.'

The five-day visit was obviously a great hit with all the ship's company for, after leaving the port and anchoring in order to embark the C-in-C of the Brazilian Navy and other VIPs, one able seaman attempted to swim from the ship back to the city. Why he was so desperate to get back will remain a mystery for after a 12-hour display by the squadrons, *Albion* returned to her berth at Praca Mava. Again the crowds flocked to visit the carrier and, apart from the fact that someone stole the Officer of the Watch's telescope on the last day, the visit to the city was a great success.

Albion left Rio de Janeiro during the morning of 3 August and, in company with the frigates *Lynx*, *Leopard* and *Chichester*, she set course for home. Two weeks later, at 3.20am on Monday 17 August 1959, the Lizard Light was sighted and that morning all the serviceable aircraft were flown off. At 7pm the same evening the Nab Tower was abeam and an hour later *Albion* anchored at Spithead to await the arrival of Customs. Finally, after all the formalities had been completed, *Albion* secured alongside the North Corner Jetty in Portsmouth Dockyard at the end of another eventful commission. She was now to undergo a four-month refit.

'Exercise Sea Demon' in the South China Sea off Manila. Here a US Navy S2F Tracker is catapulted from *Albion*.

(FAAM)

Chapter Eight

The Fourth - And Last - Commission As A Fixed-Wing Carrier

In December 1959, as the *Albion's* four-month refit was drawing near to completion in Portsmouth Dockyard, her sister ship *Bulwark* was lying nearby at Middle Slip Jetty, also in the final stages of a refit. She had undergone conversion from aircraft-carrier to commando ship, as the 'landing platform helicopters' became known, and there were strong rumours that another carrier would also be converted for this role. Although there had been no official announcement at that stage, the most likely candidate was the *Albion* as she was the only one of the six operational aircraft-carriers which had not been fitted with steam catapults in order to operate the new Sea Vixen and Scimitar aircraft. In addition, although *Albion's* deployment during 1960 was to be spent on the Far East Station, she was due to be relieved later that year which would make her readily available for conversion.

However, one thing was certain - that *Albion* would have at least one more commission as an aircraft-carrier, and on 21 September 1959 her new commanding officer, Captain F. M. A. Torrens-Spence DSO DSC AFC RN, joined her at Portsmouth. Captain Torrens-Spence was a distinguished naval aviator, having taken part in the attack on the Italian fleet at Taranto in November 1943. The recommissioning service was held in the ship's hangar at 10.45am on Monday 14 December 1959, with Earl and Lady Attlee as the guests of honour. It was the first visit that Lady Attlee had made to 'her' ship since she had launched *Albion* in 1947, and sadly it was to be her last. After the ceremony Captain Torrens-Spence and the senior officers hosted lunch for the guests, and Captain Torrens-Spence remembers both of them as, 'charming guests'. Following the ceremony the majority of the ship's company left for Christmas leave and in the first two weeks of 1960 preparations were made to ready the ship for sea.

Albion left Portsmouth during the afternoon of Monday 18 January 1960 when, with full ceremony, she slipped her berth at North Corner Jetty and left for her sea trials. As she sailed out of Portsmouth Harbour she passed the *Bulwark*, which was due to be commissioned as the Navy's first commando ship the following day. For two days the *Albion* carried out main machinery trials in the Channel, anchoring each evening in St Helens Roads off the north-east coast of the Isle of Wight, with leave being granted to the Pompey 'natives'. However, when the liberty men went to rejoin the ship early on the morning of Sunday 24 January, they found that with gale force winds blowing, the boat routine had been suspended. The *Albion* herself had been forced to move to a more sheltered berth at Spithead

Sea Venoms, Sea Hawks and Skyraiders ranged on deck. *(FAAM)*

En route to the Far East, 1960.   *(FAAM)*

and early in the afternoon Captain Torrens-Spence decided to organize an airlift to get the men back on board. With some 200 men ashore it seemed a difficult task, but fortunately a harbour tug was able to carry half that number back to the ship, and the remainder were ferried out by helicopters of 815 Squadron operating a shuttle service from the United Services football ground opposite HMS *Vernon*. Early next morning *Albion* was able to put to sea to continue her trials and at the end of that month, when they were completed, she returned to Pitch House Jetty for a long weekend and to embark the personnel of 806 (Sea Hawk) and 894 (Sea Venom) Squadrons and 894 C (Skyraider) Flight.

Albion left Portsmouth again on Tuesday 2 February 1960 and after embarking her aircraft she left home waters to work up the squadrons in the more hospitable weather conditions of the western Mediterranean. During the subsequent flying exercises there were a number of accidents which resulted in the loss of one Whirlwind, but fortunately all the aircrew were rescued without serious injuries. In mid-February there were more exercises off Malta followed by a long weekend at Messina, which gave

everyone a welcome break. On leaving the port *Albion* returned to Maltese waters where, on Saturday 27 February, she played host for the day to the Third Sea Lord, Admiral Sir J. P. L. Reid KCB CVO, who was treated to a bombing and strafing demonstration by the ship's Sea Hawk and Sea Venom aircraft. It was at this time that the First Lord of the Admiralty, Lord Carrington, announced that the Navy was to get a second commando ship in order that one could always be kept in commission. Although he would not name the ship in question, his statement that work would start in early 1961 left little doubt that, with her commission due to end in December 1960, it was the *Albion* which would join the *Bulwark* in the role.

For the first three weeks of March *Albion* was engaged in 'Exercise Starlight' off Malta, spending the weekends in Grand Harbour itself. This culminated in the inspection by FOAC,who was Rear-Admiral R. M. Smeeton MBE who, only two years previously, had been *Albion's* commanding officer. She then left the port on Monday 21 March, again wearing the flag of Rear-Admiral Smeeton, bound for Greece and a particularly important visit to Piraeus. However, at 6am on Thursday 24 March, whilst carrying out flying exercises off Malta, she received an SOS from an Italian ship, the *Giorlando*, which had lost all power and had been drifting helplessly for four days without any food supplies in a position Lat 32° - 57'N/Long 23° - 42'E, off the North African coast. After three hours hard steaming the *Albion* sighted the stricken Italian ship, and after an exchange of signals it was agreed that with skilled help from the carrier it would be possible to get the merchantman under way once again. At just after 9am one of the *Albion's* ERAs, and a delivery of food, was landed on the *Giorlando* from a Whirlwind helicopter, and after six hours' work he was able to get the Italian ship moving under her own steam. After he had returned to the *Albion*, the carrier refuelled from RFA *Tideflow* and was then able to continue her voyage to Greece.

She anchored in Piraeus Bay in the early hours of Saturday 26 March 1960, joining units of the US Sixth Fleet which were already in the port, and later that morning Divisions fell in on the flight deck. At 11.40am a 21-gun royal salute was fired and a few minutes later HRH King Paul of the Hellenes, accompanied by his son Prince Constantine, arrived on board. As he was an honorary Admiral of the Royal Navy, King Paul hoisted his flag during the visit and, after the formalities of inspecting Divisions, the two royal visitors were entertained in the wardroom, where Prince Constantine proved a very popular guest. Later that day the Greek Chief of Naval Staff and Minister of Defence both visited the ship.

When *Albion* left Piraeus Bay on the morning of Tuesday 29 March, she was bound for Port Said and the Far East Station. She embarked upon her southbound transit of the Suez Canal at 4.10am on Friday 1 April, but

Albion flying the flag of FO2 FES, exercising with HMS *Belfast* in the Far East in 1960. *(FAAM)*

Ceremonial entry into Manila Bay, 4 May 1960.

(FAAM)

at 8.32am the ship's bow hit the starboard bank of the canal and, although she did not go aground, some damage was sustained. However, she was able to steam on into the Great Bitter Lake to drop anchor so that the ship's divers could inspect the damage. Captain Torrens-Spence recalls it as a day he will never forget: 'The trouble was that my excellent navigator did not trust the canal pilot, and began to interfere with the conning of the ship. It was a case of two expert heads being worse than one and I should have put a stop to it. I might have been more alert to the danger if I had not been on the bridge during exercises for most of the time since leaving Athens. There was no question of the ship being stuck fast as she sheered off from the bank after contact with the fore part.'

In fact *Albion* was able to weigh and proceed with her voyage later that same afternoon and on Monday 4 April she berthed off Steamer Point in Aden Harbour. On leaving Aden the following day she set course for Singapore and, after a short delay in the Indian Ocean caused by a defective plummer block, she arrived alongside No 8 berth in Singapore Dockyard on the morning of Wednesday 13 April. Next day she went into King George V dry dock for repairs to her damaged bow and the ship's company were able to enjoy two weeks in the spacious comfort of HMS *Terror*.

However, by the end of the month she was at sea again and in early May, in company with the cruiser *Belfast*, the Australian destroyers *Voyager* and *Vendetta*, and US warships, she took part in annual SEATO exercises off Manila. At the conclusion of these she hoisted the flag of FO2 FES, Rear-Admiral V. A. Begg CB DSO DSC, who had transferred from the *Belfast*, and then returned to Singapore. On 17 April *Albion* departed once more, this time in company with the *Cavendish* and *Belfast*, and wearing the flag of C-in-C FES, Admiral Sir J. D. Luce KCB DSO OBE, bound for Hong Kong and Inchon in South Korea. After this the next port of call was Yokohama, which was to be the highlight of the commission, and she berthed alongside Yamashita Pier on the north side of the city at 8am on Thursday 9 June. As well as the frantic activity on the diplomatic front, with various Defence Ministry officials and VIPs visiting the ship, a party of intrepid seamen led by Sub-Lt Baller, set off on an expedition to climb Mount Fujiyama. Just over 24 hours later news was flashed to the world's Press of 'seven British sailors lost on sacred mountain'. It seems that the party of seven had, during deteriorating weather conditions, lost their way in wind and rain whilst descending the mountain. Having become overdue, experienced mountain-rescue parties were sent out but, after spending a cold, wet night huddled in a wood, the group emerged safely and travelled back to the ship by thumbing a lift and then catching a bus. At one stage, with strong winds blowing, it was thought that *Albion* might have to put to sea, but the weather stayed fine long enough for a group of Japanese VIPs to be treated to *Belfast's* Royal Marine Band beating Retreat on the carrier's floodlit flight deck.

Albion finally left Japanese waters at the end of June and returned, via Hong Kong, to Singapore where she remained until the end of July undergoing a dockyard assisted maintenance period. Early August saw the *Albion* at sea once more and, again, she was wearing the flag of FO2 FES, Rear-Admiral Michael Le-Fanu CB DSC, for fleet

HMS *Albion* in her last weeks as a fixed-wing aircraft-carrier. *(FAAM)*

exercises off the east coast of Malaya with HMS *Belfast*. Denis Burgess, who was a CPO in *Albion* at the time, recalls this period when Rear-Admiral Le-Fanu flew his flag in *Albion* and pays tribute to the Admiral who, as First Sea Lord, and in the face of fierce opposition from the RAF, saved the fixed-wing capability for the Fleet Air Arm in the form of the Sea Harrier: 'During the commission we carried the flag of FO2 FES, Rear-Admiral Michael Le-Fanu, who was a wonderful man. He spent a good deal of time in the *Albion*, where he used to walk up and down the flight deck with whoever cared to join him - from senior officers down to the most junior ratings. One evening he came to the CPO's bar and had a drink with us. He was a man with the "common touch" and his early death in November 1970 was a sad loss to the Navy.'

Following these exercises *Albion* made another visit to Hong Kong and during the afternoon of Sunday 21 August, whilst she was steaming a leisurely course through the South China Sea about 100 miles south of the colony, a signal was received requesting urgent medical assistance for a crew member of the British cargo steamer *Twinhorse*. The *Twinhorse* was about 60 miles away from *Albion* and Captain Torrens-Spence immediately increased speed to close the merchantman's position. After three hours hard steaming *Albion* was within half a mile of the *Twinhorse* and a helicopter was able to transfer a badly injured seaman back to the carrier where, in the Sick Bay, he underwent immediate surgery. Two days later, when *Albion* arrived in Hong Kong, he was transferred to hospital. In all over 20 signals were exchanged between *Albion* and the *Twinhorse*

and the final signal from the cargo ship read: 'Many thanks for your assistance. Nice to know you are just over the horizon. We think the Navy is wonderful.' From Hong Kong *Albion* steamed south to visit Subic Bay where many of the ship's company were introduced to Alongapo for the first time. After a 'never to be forgotten' five-day stop alongside SND Pier at the US Naval Base, *Albion* was at sea once again and heading through the South China Sea for Singapore. On Wednesday 14 September, the day after leaving Subic Bay, at 10.20pm during night-flying exercises, a Sea Venom crashed into the sea on take-off. Despite searches which were carried out throughout the night and until 10am the next morning, there was no trace of the aircrew, Lt R. J. Edwards RN and Sub-Lt N. A. Croad RN, and only small pieces of wreckage were recovered. On the morning of Saturday 17 September, after having flown the squadrons off to RAF Changi and the Whirlwind helicopters of 815 Squadron to the *Bulwark*, *Albion* made a full ceremonial entry into Singapore Dockyard where the rest of the month was spent undergoing self maintenance.

On Monday 3 October, once again wearing the flag of FO2 FES and in company with HMAS *Vampire* and HM Ships *Salisbury and Tenby*, *Albion* left Singapore for the last time as a conventional fixed-wing carrier and set courses for the Arabian Sea where she was to take part in 'Exercise Midlink 3' a full-scale maritime exercise by the navies of the CENTO countries. *En route* she made a nine-day call at Trincomalee and during the passage west she carried out exercises with the accompanying ships. Denis Burgess recalls one particular incident which caused a few grey hairs on board the *Albion* and probably even more to those in the *Salisbury*: 'In the early hours of one morning we were in the Indian Ocean carrying out a night-flying exercise, with *Salisbury* as our guard ship, when the silence in our mess was broken by an urgent voice piped over the ship's loudspeaker saying, "Stand by for collision forward". As our CPO's mess-deck was right forward in the bows of the ship we were all awake and on our feet in what seemed to be just seconds but, fortunately, no collision came. When the Chief Yeoman returned he told us that we had avoided a collision with the *Salisbury* by only the narrowest of margins because she had passed across our bows and right beneath the flare of the flight deck, becoming lost from view on the bridge.'

Fortunately, both *Albion* and *Salisbury* arrived safely off Karachi on Monday 24 October, where they joined US warships which were gathered for the exercise in the Arabian Sea during the first week of November. Later that month the *Albion* visited Mombasa before sailing for home on Saturday 26 November. Three days later a Sea Hawk ditched shortly after take-off, but the pilot was recovered safely and returned on board by the planeguard helicopter.

On the last day of November *Albion* was secured to a buoy in Aden Harbour for refuelling and early the following morning she left for Suez. During the passage north through the Red Sea flying exercises were carried out each day and on 7 December she made her transit of the Suez Canal and rendezvoused in the Mediterranean with the *Victorious*. The flying exercises were disrupted on Sunday 11 December when *Albion* met with violent storm force winds and heavy seas, which at one stage forced her speed to be reduced to 'slow ahead'. Next day, while she continued her westward passage, the cost of the storm was counted as the wreckage of catwalk fittings was cleared and inventories made of lost equipment. That same day the rumours which had abounded became fact, when it was officially announced that on her return to the UK, *Albion* was to be converted to a commando ship. However, as her progress towards Portsmouth continued, the thoughts of the ship's company were on 'home for Christmas', and on the morning of Thursday 15 December the squadrons were flown off to RNAS Culdrose, Brawdy and Yeovilton and at 11.07am on Saturday 17 December *Albion* secured alongside Pitch House Jetty where she was greeted by 2,000 relatives.

Later that morning main leave parties left the ship and in January 1961 she was taken over by Portsmouth Dockyard for conversion to a commando ship. *Albion's* days as an aircraft-carrier were over.

Captain C. D. Madden MVO DSC RN reads the Commissioning Warrant at the ceremony on 1 August 1962. The Guest of Honour was HRH The Duke of Edinburgh and to his left is Admiral Sir Alexander Bingley, C-in-C Portsmouth. *(FAAM)*

Chapter Nine

The Fifth Commission - 'The Old Grey Ghost'

Work started on *Albion's* conversion to a commando ship in January 1961 and continued for 18 months before she was ready for sea once again. The catapults and arrester wires were removed and additional mess-decks were provided for the Commando Group and the Commando Battery Royal Artillery which would be embarked. With the operational experience which had been gained from the *Bulwark* a number of improvements were made to the *Albion*. One of the most important of these was to enclose the mess-decks which gave the occupants far more privacy and allowed the air-conditioning to function more efficiently. The air-conditioning system itself was a great improvement on that which had been installed in the *Bulwark* and therefore offered a greater degree of comfort in tropical climates. The main galley was completely re-equipped, and on deck the Bofors anti-aircraft guns were removed from forward and aft of the island superstructure, as were those on the after gun sponsons, while the sponsons themselves were rebuilt to carry four LCAs, which were provided with their own davits. The feature which would always distinguish *Albion* from the *Bulwark* was the addition of a Type 965 long-range air search radar which was fitted at her mast-head.

On 10 April 1962 Captain C. D. Madden MVO DSC RN was appointed as the *Albion's* commanding officer and as the summer approached the conversion work neared completion. The Commissioning Ceremony took place on Wednesday 1 August 1962, as the *Albion* lay at Portsmouth's Middle Slip Jetty, and somehow the chaotic conditions which accompany every major refit had sorted themselves out by that time. The Guest of Honour was HRH The Duke of Edinburgh, who arrived on the flight deck by helicopter at 11.15 am precisely to be met by Captain Madden and Admiral Sir Alexander Bingley, the C-in-C Portsmouth. The service itself took place in the hangar and it was conducted by the Chaplain of the Fleet, after which Captain Madden read the Commissioning Warrant and the Commissioning Pennant was broken. It was a great occasion and families of the ship's company turned out in strength to make it a day to remember.

Four days later came Portsmouth's Navy Days and the *Albion*, with her hangar acting as an enormous canteen serving tea and sticky buns, was a great attraction, particularly when it rained. However, it was soon time to prepare the ship for sea, but when, during the morning of Tuesday 7 August strong winds delayed her sailing, there were those who predicted that, after over 18 months alongside, the *Albion* was stuck fast to the jetty after all.

Fortunately by the afternoon the high winds had moderated and *Albion* proved that she could still go, when she left Portsmouth for her trials.

Over the next seven days there was much activity in the Engineer's Office as all the ship's main propulsion machinery was put through its paces and, after returning to Portsmouth to rectify some faults, *Albion* steamed to Portland for the 'ship' work-up. For nine days the ship's company fired the guns at aircraft sleeves, replenished at sea with tankers and frigates, were taken in tow by all sorts of other ships, practised damage control and even greeted some 'Arabian Potentates'. The main problems came after the pre-wetting exercise, when everyone had to turn to and mop up the resultant floods. However, in early September, with the trials and work-up successfully completed, *Albion* steamed west to Lizard Point where the pilots of 845 and 846 Squadrons were able to make their first deck landings on the new commando ship. On Thursday 13 September *Albion* returned to Portsmouth's Middle Slip Jetty for a weekend break, before steaming west once again to start the 'military' work-up. This began on 18 September in Plymouth Sound, where 41 Commando Group and its vehicles were embarked and the C-in-C Plymouth, Admiral Sir Charles Madden KCB, visited the ship. From Plymouth *Albion* steamed west once more to the Lizard to await the arrival of the Wessex helicopters of 845 Squadron and the Whirlwind helicopters of 846 Squadron from Culdrose. The next two days were spent practising assault drills and deck landings in preparation for the ship's first assault landing. On Monday 24 September *Albion* carried out her first full-scale military exercise, 'Doubletake', when 41 Commando successfully assaulted the Purbeck Hills in Dorset and occupied the village of Tyneham on the south coast. Apart from dropping one of the trucks from a great height into the Channel, the exercise was completed successfully and the Royal Marines returned to Plymouth on board *Albion*, after which she sailed for Portsmouth again and secured alongside North Corner Jetty on 27 September.

During October 1962 the ship's company took foreign service leave and a number of inquisitive senior officers visited the *Albion* to see for themselves all the changes which had been made. Then on 1 November the advance parties of 41 Commando were embarked, to be followed soon afterwards by the main body and by 145 Commando Battery RA. Two days later, at 3.15pm on Saturday 3 November 1962, *Albion* left Portsmouth for the Far East Station. Despite the blustery November weather, crowds

3.15pm on Saturday 3 November 1962 and *Albion* leaves North Corner Jetty, Portsmouth, for her first commission on the Far East Station as a commando carrier.

Arrival at Gibraltar on a dull, wet, day, 6 November 1962.

'Assault Stations' off the barren rocks of Little Aden as 41 Commando are flown ashore.

A very smart entry into Aden Harbour on 21 November 1962.

'Anything You Can Do I Can Do Better'. *Albion* takes over from the *Bulwark*.

'Crossing the Line' at full speed across the Indian Ocean, 10 December 1962.

packed the Point and lined Sallyport as the commando ship steamed out of the harbour, and there were cheers and tears from relatives as *Albion* headed out through Spithead for a deployment which would keep her away from home waters for well over a year.

Next day, as she rounded Ushant, *Albion* steamed into severe gales and heavy seas which made the passage through the Bay of Biscay very bumpy indeed. However, three days after leaving Portsmouth she arrived in Gibraltar where it was pouring with rain, but at least the vino and beer tasted just as good as they had on her last visit, almost three years previously. After only two days in Gibraltar *Albion* set out across the Mediterranean Sea for warmer waters off Homs (now Khums Al), in Libya. In those days the Libyan government under King Idris was still allied to the West and Mu'ammer Muhommad al Gaddafi was a student at the University of Libya. It was here that *Albion*, and 41

Commando, were able to take part in 'Exercise Sandfly', during which a 'roving rebel band' wasencircled and destroyed. On completion of the exercise *Albion* left for Suez in order to catch a southbound convoy at Port Said, leaving behind one of 845's Wessex helicopters. The passage through the Suez Canal was slow and frustrating and it took almost two days to reach the open sea at Port Suez.

Once into the Red Sea, where the burning sun shone as hot as ever, it was found that some 350 valves in the air-conditioning system had been installed incorrectly, but after this problem had been rectified the air-conditioned mess-decks came into their own. At midday on Tuesday 20 November *Albion* arrived off the barren rocks of Little Aden where, as an exercise in the ship's assault role, 41 Commando were unceremoniously disembarked by helicopters and LCAs. Next morning at just after 8am,

Albion (to the left of the photograph) and *Bulwark* moored together off Steamer Point in Aden during November 1962.

18 December 1962, a wounded rebel prisoner is landed on board for treatment.

At anchor off Labuan with LCT alongside.

Albion entered Aden Harbour where she greeted her sister ship *Bulwark* once again and, judging by the crowds on *Bulwark's* flight deck, it seemed that they were pleased to see *Albion*. As Captain Madden approached the mooring buoys directly astern of *Bulwark*, and much to the amusement of the ship's company, the unmistakable and lively melody of 'Anything You Can Do I Can Do Better' resounded round Aden Harbour from *Albion's* flight deck tannoy. However, it was rumoured that Captain Madden's choice of music was not fully appreciated on *Bulwark's* bridge.

The next five days were spent exchanging 41 Commando for 40 Commando and taking over from the *Bulwark*, but there was still time for relaxation in the duty free shops at Steamer Point or on the beaches at Tarshyne, where they also sold the coldest lager in the Middle East. On Monday 26 October, with the change-over completed, *Bulwark* left harbour and set courses for Portsmouth. As she passed *Albion* the following signals were exchanged: *Bulwark* - 'Good luck. Over to you. Happy landings. You've got the weight.' *Albion* - 'We are grateful for all the spadework you have done. A good trip and a happy homecoming be it fog, mist, falling snow or heavy rain.' In the event *Bulwark* returned to the coldest winter since 1881 while *Albion* was to hold the weight of the Indonesian Confrontation for over 12 months.

Unfortunately, whilst manoeuvring to leave Aden Harbour, *Albion's* attendant tug *Sir Tom* capsized and sank with the loss of two lives. This accident resulted in a 24-hour delay, but by the following afternoon *Albion* was under way once again, bound for Malindi on the coast of East Africa. At noon on Saturday 1 December she anchored five miles off the coast of this beautiful part of

Kenya and the following day carried out 'Exercise First Call', with 40 Commando being landed to the north of Malindi town by the helicopters of 845 and 846 Squadrons. Next day, all the Marines having been landed, *Albion* steamed south for a brief visit to Mombasa.

She left Kilindini Harbour at 2.40pm on Tuesday 4 December bound for Singapore, with no particular urgency attached to this leg of the voyage. However, at just after midnight on Sunday 9 December a signal was received from the C-in-C FES which read, 'Proceed with all dispatch Singapore'. That night those who were off watch and turned in felt the whole ship vibrating far more than usual as down below in the boiler- and engine-rooms the engineers pushed the main propulsion machinery to its limits as *Albion* steamed flat out across the Indian Ocean, faster than she had ever gone before.

An armed revolt had broken out in the Sultanate of Brunei, and later the same day a further signal was received on board: 'Situation in Brunei still obscure, but clear that rebels are more numerous than at first supposed. They appear to hold Seria Oilfield area and coastal strip between Miri and Brunei. *Albion*, with 40 Cdo, has been diverted to Labuan and will arrive about 14 December 1962. *Albion* to call Singapore to load vehicles, land battery and replenish.'

This was the start of what was to be a major commitment for the commando ships but the political reasons behind the revolt were complicated. Approximately three-quarters of the island of Borneo forms part of the Indonesian Republic, whilst the remaining quarter, on the northern coast of the island was, in 1962, under British rule or protection. In the north-east was the colony of North Borneo or Sabah; to the west lay the oil-rich Sultanate of Brunei, while stretching along the remainder

Christmas Eve 1962 and it is 'business as usual' for *Albion*. A rebel prisoner is escorted on board by Royal Marines.

of the coast was the colony of Sarawak. Indonesian Borneo, which was also known as Kalimantan, had for centuries been administered by the Dutch as part of the Dutch East Indies until, in 1949, independence was achieved. Achmed Sukarno, Indonesia's first president, was an ardent nationalist who had long dreamed of bringing the whole island of Borneo (and for that matter Singapore and Malaya) under his country's domination. However, both the British government and Malaya under Tunku Abdul Rahman stood in his way.

During 1961 and 1962 negotiations between the Tunku, his neighbours in Sabah and Sarawak, the Sultan of Brunei and the British had been conducted with a view to forming a federation. However, in Brunei this was not a popular idea and it was here that Sukarno saw an opportunity to foment trouble, through which he could realize his ambitions. So in the early hours of 8 December, the so-called 'North Kalimantan National Army' led by a local politician, A. M. Azahari (who was safely in Manila), seized the Seria Oilfield and a small coastal strip between Miri and Brunei Town. That same day a force of Royal Marines and Gurkhas were flown from Singapore, but it soon became clear that more than two companies of troops would be required to quell the rebellion.

For four days *Albion* steamed hard across the Indian Ocean and fortunately the weather stayed fine. Despite the fact that she was driving ahead at full speed, with huge white waves rolling out from the ship's side, there was still time to enjoy the traditional 'Crossing the Line' ceremony and then at 4.20pm on Thursday 13 December a very weather-beaten *Albion* secured alongside No 8 berth in Singapore Dockyard where she stayed for five hours, just long enough to refuel and to embark another commando brigade before sailing for the coast of Borneo. At 7.30pm on Friday 14 December, just five days after receiving the first signal from Singapore, *Albion* anchored off Kuching at the western edge of Sarawak and disembarked 40 Commando and HQ 3rd Commando Brigade, who took up positions along the Indonesian border. The following day she anchored off Seria where 846 Squadron were disembarked, and within a week the rebellion had been crushed, which demonstrated to the rebels and to Sukarno that British forces were still very capable of quick and decisive intervention. Whilst *Albion* was off Brunei the Whirlwind helicopters of 846 Squadron flew off to the airport and Captain Madden authorized the Army

A close shave for 846 Squadron's senior pilot. Whirlwind 'U' crashed whilst operating from Brunei.

Whirlwind 'T' being returned to the ship by an RAF Belvedere, January 1963.

An Army Auster about to take off from *Albion's* flight deck. 'Just like the old days' for the FDO and his staff.

Alongside Singapore Dockyard's No 8 berth. *Ark Royal* is to the right.

commanders on the spot to use the helicopters as required without the necessity of referring to him.

Michael Axford, an NAM with 846 Squadron, recalls the events at that time: 'Whilst *en route* to Brunei our naval whites were replaced with jungle green uniforms, and rifle firing and helicopter exercises were carried out regularly. This brought home to us that it was the "real thing" and drill which had been practised at Culdrose soon became an everyday event. Once we were off Brunei the commandos were sent in to secure the airfield and once this was done we ground crews went in. We pitched our tents in what was to become "home" for many months, and we had to dig deep monsoon drainage ditches which was very hot work in the steaming, humid, rain forest. Fortunately a good supply of Tiger beer was at hand and it almost made the mosquitoes bearable. During our stay in Brunei we worked hard flying troops and their kit deep into the thick jungles - we could carry them in a few hours distances which would have taken them weeks hacking through the forests on foot. We relied on the *Albion* for major spares.'

Albion spent Christmas and New Year steaming up and down the coast of Brunei at 'assault stations' and always prepared for the next 'lift'. Casualties were embarked, as were prisoners, and the ship's four LCAs disappeared up river to Brunei Town. During the 26 days following her arrival off Borneo the *Albion's* helicopters flew nearly 1,200 sorties in direct support of 'A' Company, 40 Commando at Danau. Because of her frequent appearances off the coast of Borneo, generally arriving at first light, with a 'phantom-like' appearance, *Albion* quickly became known as 'The Old Grey Ghost of the Borneo Coast'.

However, on the morning of Tuesday 8 January 1963 *Albion* weighed anchor and left Brunei Bay, bound for

Singapore and a 26-day spell of self-maintenance in the dockyard which afforded her ship's company a period of respite. But as soon as the last nut and bolt was in place, *Albion* resumed her trooping role and the 1/7 Gurkha Rifles and the King's Own Yorkshire Light Infantry (KOYLI) were embarked before she sailed once more for Borneo. On the return journey a few days later the 1/2 Gurkha Rifles and the Queen's Own Highlanders were embarked and each evening the ship's company were treated to the sound of the 'pipes', both Scottish and Nepalese, on the flight deck. After disembarking the troops in Singapore *Albion* sailed for Hong Kong, and in the last week of February she tied up alongside the North Wall of the Naval Dockyard.

As always Hong Kong provided light relief, this time for some three weeks, but by the middle of March *Albion* was once again off the coast of Borneo and, to the delight of the Flight Deck Officer, the ship once again took on the role of a fixed-wing carrier, albeit in a very limited way. With their low landing speeds and short take-off runs, the Army's Austers found *Albion* made an excellent airport and that month they became regular visitors. For some weeks one could hear the FDO and his staff muttering 'just like the old days' as Austers and Beavers, and even the RAF's Pioneers, landed and took off from the flight deck. In early April *Albion* joined the frigates *Blackpool* and *Brighton* and the destroyer *Cavendish* for three days of exercises off the east coast of Malaya. However, it was only a temporary break because the Indonesian Foreign Minister had announced a policy of 'confrontation' with the 'neo-colonialist' and 'neo-imperialist' forces of Malaya which, he said, were pursuing a hostile policy towards Indonesia. In April groups of Indonesian 'volunteers' began to infiltrate

Albion at Kilindini Harbour, Mombasa, in April 1965.

Off Aden in late 1965.

High and dry in Singapore Dockyard's King George V dry dock during June 1963.

'Exercise FOTEX 63' off the east coast of Malaya. HMS *Duchess* nearest then, HMNZS *Otago*, HMAS *Quiberon*, HMS *Albion*, HMS *Cambrian*, HMS *Salisbury*, HMAS *Vendetta* and HMS *Plymouth*.

across the border into Sabah and Sarawak. This new tension kept *Albion* trooping between Singapore and Borneo for the remainder of April and for the first two weeks in May. There was some relief in the form of a dockyard assisted maintenance period, but by early July the ship was once again steaming her well-worn track between Singapore and Borneo with a short break for a four-day visit to Georgetown, Penang.

At the end of July *Albion*, for the only time during the commission, joined the rest of the Far East Fleet for a 12-day exercise 'Fotex 63', off Malaya's east coast. The exercise gave *Albion's* ship's company their first opportunity to show what the ship was capable of, and it was not long before she had to do just that when the cruiser *Lion*, flying the flag of FO2 FES, Rear-Admiral J. P. Scratchard CB DSC, had serious boiler-room trouble and Rear-Admiral Scratchard transferred his flag to *Albion*. Next to go down with machinery problems was the *Ark Royal*, and with her withdrawal from the exercise the C-in-C FES, Admiral Sir Desmond Dreyer KCB CBE DSC, hoisted his flag in *Albion*, which gave new meaning to the ship's football rallying cry of '*Albion* goes marching on'. At the end of the exercise *Albion* returned to Singapore for a long weekend before, at 7.40am on Tuesday 13 August, with the 1st

Greenjackets embarked, she left for Labuan once again for a simple troop transfer, with the Greenjackets replacing the Queen's Own Highlanders. Two days later, at 7am on 15 August, *Albion* anchored off Labuan and the transfer was completed by the end of the day. At just before 3pm the next day, shortly before *Albion* was due to weigh anchor for the passage back to Singapore, a signal was received from Labuan to the effect that an Auster had suffered an engine failure and had been forced to make an emergency landing only three minutes out from the airfield. Within minutes the SAR helicopter had been scrambled and three Wessex helicopters which were already airborne were diverted to assist in the search. In addition two of the LCAs were dispatched and, fortunately, the stricken Auster was located on a nearby beach. Having taken the crew safely on board, *Albion* was able to weigh anchor and head towards Singapore.

However, from ashore came reports of heightened political tensions with Indonesia as President Sukarno stepped up his policy of confrontation, which coincided with the arrival of a UN assessment team. *Albion* had just passed Kuching on her return journey when she received a signal ordering her to return to Brunei Bay where, the following day, half of 845 Squadron were flown ashore. On

December 1963 - typhoon in the South China Sea *en route* to Hong Kong.

18 March 1964, *Albion* passes *Victorious* as she leaves Kilindini Harbour bound for Aden with two RAF Belvederes.

passing Kuching for a second time another signal requesting naval support was received and, as a result, the Whirlwinds of 846 Squadron were flown off to Kuching and the remaining Wessex helicopters of 845 Squadron were sent to Sibu. At 5.45pm on Monday 19 August *Albion* finally arrived at Singapore Dockyard where preparations were soon under way for FO2's Harbour Inspection. Needless to say this went off without a hitch and it is worth quoting the closing remarks of Rear-Admiral Scratchard's report: 'The impression I had already gained of the first-class spirit within *Albion* was further confirmed by the Harbour Inspection.'

Apart from a nine-day break in Hong Kong, during which time the ship's evaporators helped out with the colony's chronic water shortage and 300 children were entertained on board, September was spent plying between Singapore and Borneo which gave rise to the rumour that the ship could actually find her own way through the South China Sea to Labuan. However, in October *Albion* left Singapore for a secret mission to Suez and the Mediterranean - but not for home. It had been decided to move a number of RAF Whirlwind and Belvedere helicopters from the UK to Singapore in order to relieve the *Albion's* squadrons and *Albion* herself was ordered to Port Tobruk in Libya where they could be flown on board before being transported east. The ship made her northbound passage of the Suez Canal on Friday 1 November and two days later she was anchored off the Libyan coast. With the Whirlwinds and Belvederes safely on board *Albion* weighed anchor and steamed east once again, and on Wednesday 20 November she was back in Singapore from where the RAF helicopters were able to continue the last few miles under their own power. The round voyage of 11,000 miles had been made in just 32 days and it had been a complete success, once again showing the versatility of the commando ship. During the

During the afternoon of Wednesday 15 April 1964 *Albion* arrived back in Portsmouth after having been away for 17 months. Flying her paying-off pennant she is seen passing Southsea on her way into harbour.

voyage, on 2 November, *Albion's* last remaining Whirlwind, piloted by Lt-Cdr B. Hartwell, and with Captain Madden and PO Maycock as passengers, had made the 5,000th deck landing - the date of the event reminding everyone that a year had gone by since the ship had left Portsmouth.

Albion sailed once again on 8 December, this time with the 1st KOYLI on board, together with some of the RAF Belvederes, bound, yet again, for Labuan. This time, however, once the troops had disembarked, the Whirlwinds of 846 Squadron, having been relieved by the RAF's 225 Squadron, were re-embarked, together with seven Wessex helicopters of 845 Squadron and the 1st Greenjackets. After dropping the troops in Singapore, *Albion* and the squadrons set course through a very stormy South China Sea for a Christmas and New Year visit to Hong Kong. Michael Axford recalls that the Whirlwinds of 846 Squadron were flown to Kai Tak for overhaul and, despite the fact that he and the rest of the ground crew commuted from the ship to the airport each day, the civilian staff would not let them carry out the work and so, 'we retired to their canteen and sampled the "San Mig" beer.' The rest of the ship's company were also enjoying the festivities when, on 9 January 1964, *Albion* was called away to Borneo - four days early. Once again Sukarno had intensified the 'confrontation' with increased rebel activity in Sabah, an area which had previously been very quiet, and at Sibu. On Monday 13 January 846 Squadron was landed at Tawau where, as Michael Axford recalls, '...there was a lot of jungle and we were back to sleeping in tents. This didn't go down too well as we thought our Boy Scouting days were over.' Three days later the helicopters of 845 Squadron were landed at Sibu and, once again, *Albion* was back in her support role.

Within two weeks of having landed her squadrons, world events once again shaped the course of *Albion's* commission when, in early February 1964, the government of Zanzibar was overthrown, following which there were mutinies by African troops in Tanganyika, Uganda and Kenya, and British help was requested to restore order. Although both the *Centaur* and *Victorious* were in the Middle East and the former, acting as a commando ship, took 41 Commando to Dar-es-Salaam from Aden, *Albion's* assistance was also required and so she left Singapore for Mombasa on the morning of Sunday 2 February. Leaving her squadrons behind in Borneo, she would not return to the Far East during that commission. She arrived in Kilindini Harbour during the afternoon of Sunday 9 February and immediately began embarking 45 Commando and units of the 16/5 Lancers, 814 Squadron and two RAF Belvederes from HMS *Victorious*. *Albion* was back in the role of commando ship, ready to land a fighting force at short notice. The following afternoon, with the embarkation completed, *Albion* left Kilindini Harbour and it was generally thought that the commandos would be landed and in action soon afterwards.

Fortunately there was an easing of the internal unrest in the former East African colonies and after five days at sea, mainly off Malindi where the ship's company were able to enjoy banyans on the long deserted beaches, *Albion* returned to Kilindini where 814 Squadron were able to resume their anti-submarine role aboard *Victorious*. By the end of February 45 Commando had been returned to Aden and *Albion* spent the first two weeks of March in Mombasa, where she was on hand should further trouble arise. To the great relief of the ship's company the political situation in East Africa remained quiet, and on 18 March she left Mombasa for Aden, docking there on the morning of Monday 23 March, to await the arrival of *Bulwark* that same afternoon. After two days which were spent transferring stores and equipment, including *Albion's* four LCAs and the remaining helicopters, *Bulwark* left for Singapore. Three days later, at 6pm on Saturday 28 March, *Albion* left Aden for Suez - and home.

After brief stops at Malta and Gibraltar she arrived in Plymouth Sound on the morning of Tuesday 14 April 1964 and that same evening, after receiving Customs clearance, she steamed up the Channel for Portsmouth, anchoring off Spithead at 7am the next day. For most of the morning dockyard tugs ferried hundreds of families out to the ship and that afternoon Admiral Sir Dennis Boyd presented Lt-Cdr David Burke, the CO of 846 Squadron, with the Boyd Trophy. The trophy - a silver Swordfish aircraft - is presented each year for the most outstanding contribution to naval aviation, and part of the citation read: 'In arduous conditions of tropical rain, high temperature and excessive humidity, and in spite of an almost complete lack of normal servicing facilities the squadron flew some 2,000 operational sorties over dense primary jungle. It was operating entirely on its own, usually unsupported by HMS *Albion*, from primitive shore bases.' Captain Madden himself was awarded the CBE for his service in command of the *Albion* during the arduous operations off Borneo. In his farewell address to the ship's company, Captain Madden paid tribute to the magnificent efforts made by everyone. The ship had steamed 85,000 miles, carried 12,000 troops from a variety of regiments, and her helicopters had made more than 10,000 operational sorties.

At 2.25pm the pilot boarded the ship at Spithead and just over half an hour later the 'Old Grey Ghost' was secured alongside South Railway Jetty. Soon afterwards her ship's company was broken up as the main leave parties left the ship for good. It had been a memorable commission and one which the author remembers with great affection.

January 1965 and *Albion* rolls through the Bay of Biscay to complete her work-up off Gibraltar, having been hampered by severe weather in the Channel.   *(FAAM)*

6 November 1964, *Albion* leaves Portsmouth for her sea trials. To the left of the picture is the uncompleted aircraft-carrier *Leviathan*. *(FAAM)*

Chapter Ten

The Sixth Commission - The End Of Confrontation

Just two days after her arrival back in Portsmouth from the Far East *Albion* was moved to Middle Slip Jetty, and on Sunday 10 May 1964 her new commanding officer, Captain J. H. Adams MVO RN, joined the ship. Four days later most of the ship's company arrived, although with *Albion* about to be taken over by the dockyard for a six-month refit, they were actually accommodated in Portsmouth Barracks. *Albion's* refit began on Monday 1 June, and during the time that she was in dockyard hands work was carried out to improve the vessel's efficiency in the commando role. The accommodation was extended enabling the ship to carry a larger commando group, and stowage arrangements were improved so that she could take more naval stores, which were needed to support the commandos once they were ashore.

On Monday 16 November, with the refit almost completed, basin trials were carried out and four days later, on Friday 20 November, the Commissioning Service was held in the hangar. After a final weekend alongside Middle Slip Jetty, *Albion* left Portsmouth for her sea trials. After six days of full-power, steering, manoeuvring and gunnery trials in the Channel, the ship paid a lightning visit to Dover on Sunday 29 November to renew her association with the Cinque Ports, and a reception was held on board for a number of ceremonially attired mayors and mayoresses, plus assorted aldermen, who were flown on by helicopter. There then followed ten more days of trials and work-up, mainly out of Portland, before *Albion* returned to Portsmouth's North Corner Jetty for the Christmas leave period.

Mid-January 1965 saw the *Albion* at sea once more and at Portland to embark the 22 Wessex V helicopters of 848 Squadron, which, with their twin, centrally coupled engines, were more powerful and also safer. However, severe gales were sweeping the south coast at the time and with no let-up in sight, Captain Adams obtained approval to steam south for Gibraltar on 13 January where it was hoped better weather would allow the completion of the work-up. Despite the fact that on at least one occasion a roll of 27° was recorded off Cape Finisterre and the cooks 'lost' 20 trays of chips, the Bay of Biscay itself was quite kind, but, unfortunately, the weather in the area was not much better than at home. However, Main Street, Gibraltar, provided a welcome change from Weymouth before *Albion* set sail again on Monday 1 February for the UK, where the winter gales had eased somewhat. After embarking 41 Commando the first assault exercise took place off Lizard Point in Cornwall, when the Marines

invaded the hills around Predannock Wallas. Having successfully assaulted the Cornish coast *Albion* returned home to Portsmouth where the ship's company took foreign service leave, before the vessel left the UK for her second 18-month deployment on the Far East Station.

Albion left Portsmouth at noon on Friday 12 March 1965, on a fine, blustery day, with guard and band and full ceremony. As always the Round Tower and Battery at Sallyport were packed with relatives and well-wishers waving farewell as she started her 12,000-mile voyage east where it was clear that Borneo would, once again, be her major commitment. However, this time, instead of immediately relieving her sister ship *Bulwark*, she would join her on the Far East Station, as the latter vessel was not due to leave Singapore until early July. It was to be the first time that the two commando ships had operated together east of Suez. After calling at Gibraltar *Albion* took part in 'Exercise Sandfly' off the Libyan coast and then made her southbound transit of the Suez Canal on 23 March, arriving in Aden four days later.

It had been 12 months since she had last visited this hot, barren port at the southern tip of Arabia and during this time there had been major developments on the political front. The British government had announced that the colony would be granted independence 'not later than 1968' and that Britain intended to maintain a military presence thereafter. This announcement clearly set a deadline for the attainment of nationalist aims, in particular by the National Liberation Front (NLF), which had been founded in 1963 and which was pledged to drive the British out of South Arabia by murder and intimidation, which were its two main methods of operation. In November 1964 the NLF started a campaign of terrorism in Aden which was joined, to a lesser extent, by the rival Front for the Liberation of Occupied South Yemen (FLOSY), and which continued until November 1967 when the country became independent. Even the unusually hot, even by Aden's standards, weather of March and April 1965 did nothing to curb the terrorists and the violence of those months compelled the Governor, Sir Richard Turnbull, to introduce emergency regulations. For *Albion's* ship's company perhaps the first and most obvious sign of the extra security precautions was the sight of the ship's motor whalers, manned by armed seamen, circling the ship every night while she was moored off Steamer Point. Once ashore the security became even more obvious as armed guards escorted personnel around the colony, a duty which *Albion's* own seamen's department also shared. For the pilots

A quick call at Gibraltar before returning home. *(FAAM)*

At just after midday on Friday 12 March 1965, *Albion* left Portsmouth for her second deployment as a commando ship east of Suez.   *(FAAM)*

27 March 1965, arrival at Aden with the Wessex helicopters spelling out the ship's name.　　(FAAM)

of 848 Squadron the Radfan campaign became a reality when a flight of Wessex helicopters was detached ashore in support of the Army and 45 Commando, which was to bear the brunt of the Radfan operations. During this time one of the squadron's helicopters rescued two badly wounded Marines in the rebel-infested hills near Dhala, some 40 miles north of Aden.

Following this period of activity *Albion* took part in an assault exercise, 'Jebel Jumper', with 45 Commando on the barren coastline of the Protectorate of Aden, and when she finally sailed on 8 April, after refuelling, it is doubtful whether any member of the ship's company regretted leaving the colony which had always been uncomfortable and exhausting at the best of times, but which was now dangerous, grim and frustrating, and almost intolerably restricted. *Albion* was now bound for Mombasa and on the way south she offered assistance to the 9,360-ton Clan Line passenger-cargo liner *Ayrshire*, which had been beached on

the barren island of Abd Al Kuri, off the Somalian coast. The ship had struck an uncharted rock some two weeks previously and her master had run her onto the shore to prevent her from sinking. Fortunately her passengers had already transferred to other vessels, and *Albion's* offer of help was declined.

Albion's arrival at Mombasa on 12 April was a welcome relief after Aden, although here too for a time it appeared there would be political upheaval with reports of an impending communist coup against the Kenyan government. Fortunately these fears were unfounded and the Kenyan Minister for Economic Development, Mr Tom Mboya, visited the ship where he and his family were entertained by Captain Adams. On 19 April, shortly after leaving Mombasa for her voyage east across the Indian Ocean to Singapore, a signal requesting medical assistance was received from a Russian oil tanker, *Poti*, and one of 848 Squadron's helicopters took *Albion's* MO to the Russian ship where he was able to treat an injured stoker. Four days later the ship's company got a look at Gan - another extremely isolated outpost of Empire - before proceeding to Singapore Dockyard where *Albion* berthed in the Stores Basin on Wednesday 28 April, after an absence of 14 months.

Albion's return to the Far East Station coincided with Indonesia's most ambitious venture of the Borneo campaign, a direct attack on an Army base situated on a hilltop at Plamam Mapu in the First Division of Sarawak, near Kuching. The 'confrontation' with Indonesia was still a long way from being resolved and *Albion* was soon back on her well-worn route between Singapore and the north coast of Borneo. In early May she conveyed 42 Commando to Tawau and then, after a 12-day self-maintenance period at Singapore Dockyard, she sailed for Sibu where 848 Squadron were disembarked as they went ashore to relieve 845 Squadron, who were due to return home to Culdrose in the *Bulwark*. Whilst *Albion* was off Borneo the SRN5 Hovercraft carried out some limited trials from the ship, transporting troops and carrying stores ashore. However, more extensive trials were eventually cancelled. Meanwhile, *Albion*, wearing the flag of C-in-C FES, steamed north for Hong Kong where she arrived on Sunday 30 May, and where some of the younger members of the ship's company were introduced to the delights of Wanchai for the first time. Unfortunately the visit was cut short on Friday 4 June when reports of a typhoon were received, and so *Albion* left to ply her familiar route between Singapore and Borneo. Once more the 'Old Grey Ghost' renewed her acquaintanceship with Labuan, Jessleton (now Kota Kinabalu), Sibu, Tawau and Kuching, not to mention all the Army regiments whose names had been so familiar during 1963. Another word even entered the ship's company's vocabulary - roulement - army jargon used when rotating troops on the front line. In the previous

A Royal Marine band to welcome her alongside at Singapore on 28 April 1965.
(FAAM)

SRN5 Hovercraft trials off Borneo in May 1965. *(FAAM)*

Leaving Singapore for 'Exercise Goldplate'. (FAAM)

Albion refuels at sea, late October 1965. *(FAAM)*

commission these operations had simply been known as troop transfers. *Albion's* operations off Borneo continued for the best part of June, July, August and September, with a break for maintenance during July when *Bulwark* left Singapore for Australia and home.

In early October, following their granting of independence, Sarawak and Sabah elected to join the Federation of Malaysia, an event which incensed Sukarno who promised 'terrible confrontation', and roused the mobs of Jakarta into furious rioting during which the British Embassy was sacked and burned. However, despite the increased tension, *Albion* was relieved from duty in South-East Asia and she steamed west to visit the Seychelles, then Mombasa for a week-long self-maintenance period. Following this it was back to Aden, on more than one occasion, where the political tensions were much the same as they had been just over six months previously, and once again no one was very sorry to leave. *Albion* also visited two new ports at this time, Assab in Ethiopia and Djibouti in the French colony of that name, which was described as being 'similar to Aden, but without the bombs'.

Albion finally said goodbye to Aden on 25 November to return to her former haunts off Borneo. On 18 December the helicopters of 848 Squadron flew 42 Commando into the First Division of Sarawak for their fifth operational tour

in North Borneo, as they replaced 2/2 King Edward VIIs Own Gurkha Rifles. It was during this operation that the squadron suffered its only fatal accident of the commission, when one of its helicopters crashed, killing the pilot, Lt Bruce Brown RN, his co-pilot Sub-Lt T. J. H. Wotton RN, two midshipmen and one of the squadron's petty officers. Their funerals were held in the military cemetery at Singapore. Christmas 1965 was spent in Singapore, with a carol service held on the flight deck and attended by the C-in-C FES and the Naval Base choir. Another highlight was a children's party for 100 underprivileged youngsters which was organized by Sub-Lt Peter Waites and an enthusiastic band of 'pirate' helpers. Father Christmas who, true to form, arrived complete with thick white beard and red robes, was just saved from a complete melt-down in his heavy costume by the timely donation of some iced Tiger beer. Although *Albion* spent New Year's Eve alongside in Singapore Dockyard, she sailed for Hong Kong the following morning - complete with a few hundred hangovers. She arrived alongside Hong Kong Dockyard's North Arm on 5 January 1966 for a ten-day 'rest & recreation' visit which, as always, proved very popular. On 12 January Captain B. C. G. Place VC DSO RN took command of the *Albion* from Rear-Admiral Adams, who was leaving the ship upon his promotion. As he was towed

Celebrations in the Red Sea as *Bulwark* 'takes the weight', August 1966. *(FAAM)*

Resisting all temptations to carry out full power trials in the Suez Canal, *Albion* makes her final transit of the waterway on 31 August 1966.

(FAAM)

Eight days after leaving Port Said *Albion* arrives at Portsmouth.

into HMS *Tamar* in the ship's Land Rover by the senior officers he was given a rousing send-off, particularly by Jenny's Side Party who let off strings of ear-splitting Chinese firecrackers.

Albion's new commanding officer, Captain Godfrey Place VC, had entered Dartmouth at 18 years of age in 1939 and in 1941, after volunteering for submarines, he was appointed to the 10th Submarine Flotilla where he was awarded the DSC and the Polish Cross of Valour for his service as a liaison officer with the Polish submarine *Sokol*. Early in 1943 he was appointed to the 12th Submarine Flotilla which consisted of midget submarines (X-craft). In September 1943, whilst commanding *X7*, Lt Place took part in the attack on the German battleship *Tirpitz* and despite enormous difficulties, he pressed home his attack which resulted in the *Tirpitz* being seriously damaged and finally incapacitated. For this action Lt Place and Lt Cameron, who had commanded *X6*, the only other midget submarine to press home the attack, were both awarded the VC.

After leaving Hong Kong the *Albion* returned to Borneo before steaming to Singapore at the end of February for a dockyard assisted maintenance period, during which time the ship's company moved into the 'luxury' accommodation of HMS *Terror*. With the refit completed, *Albion* left Singapore on 20 April for her shakedown trials which took her up the east coast of Malaya, where the banyan fans were able to enjoy Pulau Tioman. However, this change in the ship's routine did not last for long and she soon returned to Labuan to carry out a troop transfer.

On 11 May, with the end of the commission in sight, *Albion* sailed for Kobe in Japan and then Borneo once again. Then came a spell of maintenance at Singapore and after 'Exercise Long Hop', a visit to Hong Kong in July. After farewell visits to Borneo and Hong Kong, *Albion* steamed west once again, this time bound for Suez. On 11 August, shortly before *Albion* sailed for home, a peace agreement was signed in Jakarta which signalled the end of the 'confrontation' with Indonesia. On 30 August 1966, whilst in the Red Sea, she rendezvoused with the *Bulwark* and, after exchanging some stores, *Albion* set course for home and *Bulwark* for Singapore. Any temptations to carry our a full power trial in the Suez Canal were resisted, and *Albion* arrived in Portsmouth Harbour on Thursday 8 September 1966. It had been another eventful commission during which she had steamed 88,000 miles, and had operated with all five commando units, together with several infantry battalions. During the commission, in addition to her normal flying, *Albion* had continued to operate the small fixed-wing aircraft and by May 1966 there had been more than 70 landings by Army Air Corps Austers and Beavers, and RAF Pioneers. With no arrester wires or barriers there were limitations to the numbers which could be landed at any one time, but the Austers really made themselves at home by joining the helicopters down in the hangar.

Now *Albion* was to undergo a 17-week refit before her next commission.

Chapter Eleven

The Seventh Commission - Departure From Aden

After her refit *Albion* recommissioned at Portsmouth on Thursday 6 April 1967 and the Guest of Honour was General Sir Norman H. Tailyour, the Commandant General Royal Marines. The Commissioning Warrant was read by Captain Place and after the service conducted by the Chaplain of the Fleet, the commissioning cake was cut by Mrs Place. The weather that day was dull and windy and the ceremony was held in the after hangar with over 500 relatives and friends of the new ship's company taking the opportunity to attend and look over the ship.

The following forenoon *Albion* sailed from Portsmouth into heavy rain, high winds and rough seas, in order to carry out her post-refit trials, and during the next few days 848 Squadron returned to the ship from their winter retreat at Culdrose. The voyage north through the Irish Sea in early May was dogged by atrocious weather but, flying the flag of the C-in-C Plymouth, *Albion* visited Liverpool to commemorate the Battle of the Atlantic. Despite the dismal weather *Albion's* arrival alongside Princes Landing Stage was heralded by an impressive 16-aircraft fly-past by 848 Squadron, and even though Liverpool were playing at home, 10,000 visitors toured the ship during two open days. After a memorable weekend in Liverpool *Albion* began her work-up exercises in earnest, with 41 Commando and 145 Battery Royal Artillery. The Marines assaulted the coast

at Weymouth, and they landed on Bodmin Moor before re-embarking for full-scale exercises in Northern Ireland and Scotland. The idyllic peace of Red Bay, Cushendall, Co Antrim, was shattered by the arrival of 41 Commando and later the small town played host to the ship's company, who managed to consume all the Guinness in the local hostelries. From there *Albion* steamed north to the Western Isles and 'Exercise Dry Fly II', which was designed to test sea assault strategies. But hardly had the exercise begun than *Albion* was ordered back to Portsmouth 'with all dispatch' as, once again, world events were about to chart the course of the ship's career.

In late May 1967 there were serious political tensions building up in the Middle East between Israel and her Arab neighbours, and Egypt had banned Israeli ships from using the Gulf of Aqaba. As the tensions increased, ships of the US Sixth Fleet and the Royal Navy's Mediterranean Fleet were sent to the eastern Mediterranean, where the presence of Soviet ships from the Black Sea Fleet did not help matters. Therefore, when *Albion* left Portsmouth on Wednesday 31 May it was widely assumed by the world's Press that she too was steaming for Malta. There was even speculation that Britain and the US were planning to intervene in the Middle East and occupy the Suez Canal zone. When *Albion* called at Gibraltar for six hours during the early morning of Saturday 3 June and then steamed

On Thursday 7 September 1967 *Albion* left Portsmouth for the Far East. This time she would not return until July 1969.

The naval task force arrive at Aden. HMS *Fearless* leads the column with the *Triumph* and *Sir Bedivere* following and *Albion* about to form up into line ahead.

Full power trials January 1968.

The withdrawal from Aden. *Albion* anchored off Steamer Point with RFA *Stromness*.   *(FAAM)*

Towing exercise during the work-up in the South China Sea, January 1968. An RFA tries to get a little too friendly.
(FAAM)

back into the Atlantic and set course for the south-west there was even more speculation. An MoD denial that *Albion* was to be in any way involved in the Middle East crisis and that she would be undertaking 'operations in the Atlantic' did nothing to dampen the Press theories. One newspaper even predicted that she would arrive in the Red Sea on 19 July 1967. However, the outbreak of the Arab-Israeli Six-Day War on 6 June pushed the *Albion* out of the headlines. In fact the 'Old Grey Ghost' was, as the MoD had said, involved in the Atlantic Ocean and the Red Sea was not to be her destination.

On 30 May 1967 a civil war had erupted in the former British colony of Nigeria, caused by the secession of the eastern region of Biafra from the Nigerian Federation. The British government were very concerned for the safety of the large numbers of Britons in that country, and the *Albion* had been ordered to take up station off the Nigerian coast in case it became necessary to evacuate British nationals. The secrecy surrounding the mission was essential as the Commando Brigade and the Royal Artillery Battery were, if necessary, prepared to land ashore in order to establish a bridgehead for the proposed evacuation. Petty Officer Robin Williams recalls, '...two occasions when the ship's Wasp helicopters, blacked out and with all identification markings removed, brought British Embassy officials on board from the mainland for briefings with Captain Place

and Lt-Colonel Patrick Ovens, the CO of 41 Commando, but most days were spent cruising slowly just over the horizon from Lagos and the island of Fernando Po. At times the temperatures in the upper parts of the boiler-rooms were so high that we had to scale the ladders whilst holding our breath, otherwise it burned the lungs.'

As Petty Officer Terry Higgins recalls: 'Once our destination became known we all had to have various vaccinations and pull out our tropical kit. During our time off Africa the weather was hot and, with very little flying being done, the flight deck took on the appearance of Blackpool Promenade, but with much more sun. During the days we remained off the coast there was little to relieve the monotony and we ran sweepstakes with cash prizes for those who guessed correctly the day we would return home. Finally, early in July, we headed north once again and we arrived back in Portsmouth on Wednesday 5 July 1967.' Fortunately, *Albion's* services had not been required, and for the ship's company it had been an unusual and unexpected interlude.

During July and August *Albion* remained at Portsmouth where leave was taken by the ship's company and the daily routine was enlivened by a visit from Billy Smart's Circus. Despite some very windy weather the performers entertained the ship's company on the flight deck and soon afterwards, during Portsmouth's Navy Days, the ship's

At Hong Kong for Chinese New Year, February 1968. *(FAAM)*

Chipping away at the flight deck. Hong Kong February 1968, with the old China Fleet Club in the background.

Indian Ocean 1968. *(FAAM)*

A full flight deck May 1968. *(FAAM)*

company played host to some 38,000 visitors who toured the vessel. Finally, at 3pm on Thursday 7 September 1967 *Albion* left Portsmouth bound once again for the Far East Station although this time, with the Suez Canal closed, she was routed by way of South Africa. However, before heading south she carried out a final exercise with 41 Commando off South Wales and it was Wednesday 13 September when she left UK waters. On 26 September *Albion* rounded the Cape of Good Hope and soon afterwards she arrived in Durban, a port which she had last visited in June 1959. She was the first major British warship to visit the city for some years and the 'Lady in White', Mrs Perla Gibson, was there to sing her in. During the visit the local population provided almost overwhelming hospitality, and a full range of social activities was held on board in the form of children's parties, cocktail parties and the opening of the ship to visitors. Upon leaving the port Captain Place invited Mrs Gibson and her companion on board to the flight deck to 'sing' the *Albion* out of harbour. They were then returned ashore in the ship's Wasp helicopter. After leaving Durban, *Albion* steamed north for Aden where there would be no

hospitality, only hostility.

Albion arrived off Aden, in company with HMS *Phoebe* and RFA *Lyness*, during the night of Wednesday 11 October and, at 4.30am, she rendezvoused with the *Bulwark* which had landed 42 Commando at Steamer Point the previous day. On Friday 13 October *Albion* anchored off Aden's Steamer Point and began a routine which was to become very familiar during the following eight weeks.

Since *Albion's* last call at Aden in August 1966, the political situation in the colony had deteriorated still further. The Israeli victory in the six-day conflict in June that year had increased the nationalist fervour in Aden and it had hastened the disintegration of the Federal Government which was already demoralized by the NLF's regime of murder and intimidation, and by the pending withdrawal of British support. At the end of June Middle East Command was given 20 November 1967 as the date for the final withdrawal from Aden, the day on which the colony would become independent. However, British forces still had to endure five months of raging terrorism and this was the situation to which *Albion* returned.

Terry Higgins clearly remembers those days: 'We anchored off Steamer Point on 13 October and although we were told that the political situation was quiet, there was little relaxation. *Albion's* helicopters flew continuous patrols in support of 42 Commando, and we were not allowed ashore. Security was tight for the few British residents that were left in the colony and they were only allowed to go to the shops at Steamer Point, which were heavily guarded, for a few hours in the morning and afternoon.' By this time 45 Commando had withdrawn to a line which covered the neck of the isthmus and protected the airfield at Khormaksar. Meanwhile, 42 Commando had taken over security duties at Tawahi, Maalla and Steamer Point, supported by the Wessex Vs of 848 Squadron which had taken on a more aggressive appearance with a GPMG mounted in the starboard window. In early November, with the NLF fast winning the battle against its rival FLOSY, the British trained South Arabian Army threw in its lot with the former organization, and all that remained was for Sir Humphrey Trevelean, the last Governor, to hand over any power that he still had. At about this time the withdrawal date, popularly known as 'W' Day, was changed to 29 November and in the week beforehand the RAF carried out a massive airlift of personnel from Khormaksar, leaving only 42 and 45 Commandos supported by the *Albion* to maintain security around Steamer Point. Outside Aden a naval task force, which included the *Eagle, Albion, Fearless, Triumph, Intrepid, London* and *Ajax,* and which was commanded by Rear-Admiral Edward Ashmore CB DSC, stood by and on 25 November Sir Humphrey Trevelean embarked in HMS *Appleton* to review the fleet of 24 ships. This was followed by fly-pasts of *Eagle's* fixed-wing aircraft and *Albion's* helicopters.

On 28 November 42 Commando were withdrawn from Steamer Point, after which they took up defensive positions around Khormaksar Airfield, and at the same time 45 Commando were flown out to various ships of the task force. The same day Sir Humphrey Trevelean stood on the steps of the aircraft which was to fly him back to the UK while *Eagle's* Royal Marine Band struck up 'Fings Ain't Wot They Used To Be' which, in the circumstances, seemed very appropriate. For the final 24 hours of British rule in Aden 120 men of 42 Commando, commanded by Lt-Col 'Dai' Morgan, held the final perimeter before they too were evacuated the next day. The last British serviceman to leave Aden was Lt-Col Morgan who was flown out at 3pm after formally handing over command to Rear-Admiral Ashmore, thus bringing to an end 128 years of British rule. Between 1947 and 1970 these final departures from former British colonies had become a fairly frequent occurrence for British servicemen and they were usually accompanied by a certain amount of regret and nostalgia. However, it is doubtful whether any British serviceman, from the C-in-C

downwards, ever regretted leaving Aden. During the 48 days that 848 Squadron had supported the commando unit ashore they flew 7,144 sorties and delivered almost £2½ million worth of stores, consisting of everything from ammunition to ice-cream. It was an impressive feat by both the pilots and the maintenance crews.

The ships of the task force remained in Aden's territorial waters for a further nine hours until midnight, when South Arabia became officially independent, and in the early hours of 30 November *Albion* left the area and set course for Singapore. She arrived at the Naval Base on Friday 15 December 1967 after 73 days at sea, and just in time for a monsoon deluge. As the *Albion* was taken into dockyard hands for a maintenance period, the ship's company were, at last, able to relax. On Christmas Eve there came a change of command when Captain M. S. Ollivant MBE DSC RN took over from Rear-Admiral Place, who left for the UK on promotion.

Now that the confrontation with Indonesia was over, *Albion's* third Far Eastern deployment as a commando ship was far more relaxed and at the end of January 1968 she made a six-day visit to Hong Kong, before returning to Singapore and dry docking for more maintenance. *Albion* was at sea again in early April and just over a week later she was sent west across the Indian Ocean on another secret mission. She had been ordered to stand by off Aden in case she was required to evacuate the few remaining British nationals left in the country which, after the withdrawal of British forces, had slid into civil war. Fortunately, her services were not required and the mission ended at Gan.

In May she took part in 'Exercise Quickjump' and followed this, in June, with a very popular maintenance period at Hong Kong which, in turn, was followed by a successful inspection by Vice-Admiral Ashmore, FO2 FES. Later that month 848 Squadron took part in 'Exercise Lath' and in July the ship made an 11-day visit to Fremantle where the lasting memory of most members of the ship's company was the overwhelming hospitality shown to them by the local people, and the ship's dance, held in the city's Pagoda Ballroom. In September *Albion* took part in 'Exercise Coral Sands' which involved 50 ships of the RN as well as the US Navy, RAN and RNZN including HMS *Hermes,* HMAS *Sydney* and HMS *Triumph* and HMNZS *Waikato.* For a fortnight two fleets battled with each other and at the conclusion of the exercise came another very popular visit of the commission, to Brisbane.

By this time the commission was drawing to a close and members of the advance party were joining the ship in order to find their way around. *Albion* was due to recommission at Singapore and once the ship returned to the Naval Base in early November over half the ship's company flew home to Brize Norton. For the first, and the last, time in her career *Albion's* commission had ended whilst the ship was overseas.

Pilot's eye view of *Albion. (FAAM)*

Chapter Twelve

The Eighth Commission - Departure From Singapore And The Final Years

HMS *Albion* recommissioned at Singapore on 25 November 1968 and left for her work-up in the South China Sea in early December, before returning to Singapore. On 11 December she hoisted the flag of Vice-Admiral Anthony T. Griffin CB, FO2 FES, and steamed north-east across the Gulf of Thailand to Cambodia and Sihanoukville (now Kompong Som), where she was the first British warship to visit the country for eight years. Although the government of Prince Sihanouk was in power, there was evidence that insurgents led by the notorious Pol Pot were active when Vice-Admiral Griffin and Captain Ollivant made an official visit to the ancient city of Angkor, accompanied by heavily armed guards. Captain Ollivant recalls that instead of martial music, the Royal Marine Band played 'soft shoe shuffle' tunes to VIPs

at the official reception and this was very well received. The visit to Cambodia lasted just three days after which *Albion* returned to Singapore, where she spent Christmas and the New Year.

On 20 March 1969 Vice-Admiral Griffin again hoisted his flag in *Albion* and the ship steamed north through the South China Sea to Hong Kong, then on through the East China Sea and the Yellow Sea to Inchon in South Korea. On 10 April Vice-Admiral Griffin and Captain Ollivant made an official visit to the hillside memorial in honour of the 1st Battalion The Gloucestershire Regiment and C Troop, 170 Battery Royal Artillery, who made a heroic stand at the Battle of Solma-Ri in April 1951. It was a vital delaying action in the Battle of the Imjin River and the memorial on 'Gloucester Hill', as it became known to the

Albion recommissions at Singapore on 25 November 1968. Captain Martin Ollivant reads the Commissioning Warrant.

(FAAM)

July 1969, *Albion* calls at Port Louis, Mauritius, on her way home via the Cape of Good Hope.　　　*(FAAM)*

'Exercise Clockwork 71'. *Albion* in Arctic waters near Harstad.　　　*(FAAM)*

Albion approaches Singapore Dockyard on 12 May 1971 during her final deployment on the Far East Station. 848 Squadron provides a fly-past. *(FAAM)*

Leaving Fremantle on 17 August 1971 after a ten-day 'winter' visit. *(FAAM)*

British Army, was constructed with the help of schoolchildren from the nearby village of Solma-Ri. After laying a wreath there *Albion's* two naval officers inspected a guard of the South Korean Army.

The *Albion's* next port of call was Kobe in Japan, after which she returned to Singapore where, on 28 April, FO2 FES struck his flag. In May the ship visited Fremantle before taking her leave of Singapore in early June to return to the UK, via the Cape of Good Hope. On 7 July she called at Port Louis, Mauritius, where two 4-ton cannon were loaded for the voyage home. They had been salvaged from an old British warship which had been sunk off Mauritius by the Dutch and had been used in Port Louis as street barriers. Having been offered to the city of Portsmouth for their display of ordnance at Southsea Castle Museum, the cannon were presented to Captain Ollivant by the Mayor of St Louis, and after leaving Mauritius *Albion* called at Durban, sailing on 14 July for a non-stop passage to Portsmouth.

Albion entered Portsmouth Harbour early in the afternoon of Wednesday 30 July 1969, after 22 months east of Suez. Over 1,00 relatives were taken out to Spithead to travel the last few miles home with the ship. Lt-Cdr D. C. Allen RN and seven other members of the ship's company formed an unusual saluting party when, dressed in Nelsonian rig, they fired a 13-'cannon' salute to the C-in-C Portsmouth. As *Albion* was secured alongside she was greeted by 500 more relatives and the Royal Marine Band from HMS *Hermes*. Since leaving Portsmouth in September 1967 she had steamed 109,580 miles and the Wessex V helicopters of 848 Squadron had flown 8,334 hours. Ahead of her lay an eight-month refit and her final deployment east of Suez.

On 3 March 1970 Captain H. C. Leach RN took over command from Captain Martin Ollivant, and just over a month later, on 8 April, Captain Leach renewed the ship's affiliation with the Cinque Ports when all the members met at Hastings in their 'Courts of Brotherhood and Guestling'. This entailed attending a church service, marching through the streets of the town, sitting through the ceremony and then, at the end of a long lunch, making a speech to the assembled mayors and guests. One week later, at 3pm on Wednesday 15 April, *Albion* left a mist shrouded Portsmouth Harbour for her sea trials in the Channel and in the following month, flying the flag of Vice-Admiral Sir Anthony Griffin CB, who was now C-in-C Plymouth, she formed the main naval presence at Liverpool for the annual Battle of the Atlantic remembrance week. At the time there was a dockers' strike at the port and Captain Leach had to get his ship alongside Princes Pier with a 'roaring' tide without the aid of tugs. He described it as, 'Quite a testing experience'. In August *Albion* visited Wilhelmshaven, before exercising off the east coast of Scotland and visiting Scapa Flow. In September she went to Greenock where she was weather-bound during storms, but later in the month she exchanged these conditions for the more settled weather of the eastern Mediterranean during amphibious landing exercises with 42 Commando. During this period she visited Malta and in early November she took part in joint exercises with French naval units off Corsica. She returned to Portsmouth in December 1970, in time for Christmas and New Year celebrations and to undertake a short maintenance period.

On 5 January 1971 there was another change of leaders

The withdrawal from Singapore, 2 November 1971. Organized chaos on the flight deck. *(FAAM)*

109

The Royal Navy's Guard, mainly provided by *Albion's* ship's company, for the final parade before the C-in-C Far East. *(FAAM)*

when Captain J. G. Jungius RN took command. Once again over half of the ship's company had changed, and on 28 January 1971 *Albion* left Portsmouth for Lizard Point where she embarked the Wessex V helicopters of 845 Squadron and then undertook a few days' work-up in the Channel. February 1971 found *Albion* steaming for Norwegian waters and 'Exercise Clockwork 71' which was to take place in the Arctic around the Lofoten Isles. 45 Commando were embarked off Harstad and during the following week mini assaults were carried out on the snow covered Norwegian coast. On board, to cope with the Arctic weather, a special 'snow-plough' was constructed from one of the fork lift trucks for use on the flight deck, but it was never as efficient as members of the ship's company armed with shovels. Fortunately, after a week or so of these conditions *Albion* returned to Portsmouth to undergo a dockyard assisted maintenance period before setting out on her final Far Eastern deployment.

In December 1967, the Labour government which, like all previous Labour administrations, was reluctant to spend money on defence, was faced with a massive financial crisis which led to the devaluation of sterling. Huge public spending cuts were required and it was proposed that £100 million be removed from the defence budget. However, the only way this could be done was to withdraw from the bases in Malaysia and the Persian Gulf within the next few years and concentrate the Armed Forces in Europe and the North Atlantic. The decision was severely criticized by the Conservative Opposition as a 'scuttle' from east of Suez, but Edward Heath's administration of 1970-74 did nothing

to reverse the situation. The political reality was that Britain's future lay with Europe and not east of Suez, and the *Albion* was to play her part in the withdrawal from South-East Asia.

At 11.30am on Thursday 25 March 1971 *Albion* left Portsmouth for her voyage south, but unfortunately she suffered a very sick plummer block bearing and 24 hours later she was back alongside. To save time 848 Squadron were embarked in Portsmouth and *Albion* was eventually able to leave at the end of the month and join the frigates *Achilles* and *Danae*. The remaining aircraft joined the ship off Portland and courses were set for Ushant and Biscay. On her way south *Albion* made a brief stop off Ascension Island and at the Cape of Good Hope a South African Air Force Shackleton delivered some long-awaited mail.

Albion's first call was Durban where, as always, the local population provided its renowned and almost overwhelming hospitality. The visit included a full programme of social activities and the ship reciprocated with a children's party, a cocktail party and an open day, when long queues formed on the jetty as eager visitors waited for the chance to tour the ship. There was some sadness when the ship left Durban, but also some anticipation that South Africa might provide a port of call on the way home at the end of the year, as the Suez Canal showed no signs of reopening. During *Albion's* passage across the Indian Ocean, King Neptune distributed 'Crossing the Line' certificates and a brief call was made at Gan to embark Rear-Admiral D. Williams FO2 FES, who flew on by Wessex helicopter and hoisted his flag for the

8 November 1971 and *Albion* steams round Singapore's south coast for the last time. *(FAAM)*

The withdrawal from Singapore and the final steam-past. HMS *Triumph* is astern of the *Albion* and 848 Squadron's helicopters provide the main section of the fly-past. *(FAAM)*

Albion, complete with Union Flag painted on the flight deck, refuels from RFA *Tidereach* during the weeks she spent in the Bay of Bengal in December 1971. *(FAAM)*

May 1972 and *Albion* takes part in 'Exercise Dawn Patrol' in the eastern Mediterranean. In the background is the USS *Guadalcanal.*

Albion, with the Wessex V helicopters of 848 Squadron ranged on deck *(FAAM)*

second of *Albion's* ports of call, Bombay. It was the first time that the ship had been to the port since those early days in February 1956 and, indeed, this visit of *Albion's* was the first by a British warship for some time.

From Bombay *Albion* steamed east across the Bay of Bengal, arriving off Singapore on 12 May. Here the peace which had reigned on board while the ship's company had the whole ship to themselves was shattered, when she was suddenly invaded by 40 Commando who were embarked by helicopter, and the familiar long queues formed all over the vessel. They were on board to carry out a counter-terrorist operation, 'Exercise New Look II', in Brunei and once again the *Albion* became 'The Old Grey Ghost of the Borneo Coast'.

On 22 May, with the exercise completed, *Albion* made a ceremonial entry into Singapore Naval Base, with 848 Squadron providing a fly-past as they departed to Simbang. The *Albion* then spent a month alongside No 8 berth in the Stores Basin as she underwent an assisted maintenance period which ended in late June, after which she sailed for Kobe in Japan, complete with an Australian Army Band. *Albion* went alongside in Kobe on 1 July and she spent a week in the port before returning for a weekend at

Singapore where she re-embarked 40 Commando. In company with the *Intrepid, Otago, Jaguar, Danae, Achilles* and the RFAs *Tidepool* and *Tarbatness*, *Albion* sailed from Singapore and up the east coast of the Malayan peninsula to the Marang area, where she took part in 'Exercise Round Up'. This was designed to test the complexities of a night assault and on completion *Albion* returned to Singapore.

In early August *Albion* sailed south through some very severe weather and rough seas to make a 'winter' visit to Fremantle for seven hectic days. Once again the Aussies provided overwhelming hospitality and the arrival in Singapore on 23 August provided a welcome break for some, and a few weeks' maintenance for the ship. *Albion* left Singapore on 20 September and after crossing the South China Sea she paid a two-day visit to Subic Bay, where the unique attractions of Olangapo left indelible memories for many of the ship's company. From the US Naval Base at Subic Bay *Albion* steamed north into the South China Sea and, just avoiding a typhoon, she arrived in Hong Kong for a farewell visit on 30 September. For ten days, or until their money ran out, some made the most of the floating restaurants of Aberdeen or the bars of Wanchai, whilst others preferred touring the New Territories and

In June 1972 *Albion* was at Rosyth where she received a visit from the Grand Duke of Luxembourg. She also embarked 848 Squadron and 45 Commando.

(FAAM)

In July 1972 *Albion* made her farewell visit to Dover where choppy seas prevented an open day, but the civic dignitaries were able to say goodbye to the ship which had been adopted by the Confederation of the Cinque Ports nearly 19 years earlier.

(FotoFlite)

swimming at Repulse Bay.

In June 1970 the *Hermes* had finished her last commission as a fixed-wing carrier and it was decided to convert her at Devonport for the commando ship role. It was widely assumed that she would replace the 'ageing' *Bulwark*, but in the autumn of 1971 it became clear that she would, in fact, take over from the *Albion* which was to be withdrawn from operational service in late 1972.

When *Albion* returned to Singapore Naval Base on 15 October there followed an extremely busy two weeks of storing ship, embarking the whole of 40 Commando and the Sphinx Battery, Royal Artillery and generally preparing for the Royal Navy's withdrawal from the Singapore base, just 34 years after it had been opened by the then Governor of Singapore, Sir Shenton Thomas. The Farewell Parade for the C-in-C Far East, Air Chief Marshal Sir Brian Burnett, was held at 5.30pm on 29 October 1971 at Sembawang and all the Armed Forces were represented by colour guards, with *Albion* providing the major part of the Naval Guard, together with the Guard Commander, Lt T. H. Brown RN and the Colour Officer, Lt G. Bateman RN. The fly-past was led by 848 Squadron and 40 Commando provided the

Royal Marines Guard. It was a sad occasion but the political fact was that Britain was moving closer to Europe and had almost completed its withdrawal from Empire. On 31 October, with the official hand-over of the Naval Base to the ANZUK Forces completed, *Albion* formed part of a 20-ship 'steam-past' led by HMS *Glamorgan* bearing FO2 FES, Rear-Admiral D. Williams. The Fleet was reviewed by the C-in-C Far East in RFA *Stromness*, with 848 Squadron once again providing the main section of a fly-past by 30 helicopters. Later that day *Albion* left the waters around Singapore for good.

After carrying out 'Exercise Curtain Call' off Penang, *Albion* steamed west across the Indian Ocean for Gan, where mail was embarked, and Mombasa. On the way she was able to assist the Admiralty tug *Advice* which had developed an engine-room fire, but this was soon extinguished and on 14 November *Albion* arrived in Kilindini Harbour, Mombasa, for an eight-day period of self maintenance. This break provided the more adventurous with the chance to go on tours of the safari parks or to enjoy the NAAFI-run Silversands camp just north of the city. For the souvenir hunters there were

In September 1972 the ship took part in 'Exercise Strong Express' in northern Norway. During the exercise she embarked Sea King helicopters of 826 Naval Anti-Submarine Squadron. She is seen here in the Fjords near the Lofoten Islands.

Overlooked by the famous Chateau Fronternac, *Albion* leaves Quebec on the start of her final voyage to the UK after her deployment to Canada. She was, at that time, the largest warship ever to sail up the St Lawrence River to Montreal.

(FAAM)

On 24 November 1972, with a fly-past of naval helicopters paying tribute to her, *Albion* returns to Portsmouth for the last time. *(FAAM)*

On the morning of Monday 22 October 1973 a small group of well-wishers on the Round Tower wave farewell to the *Albion* as she leaves Portsmouth under tow for her final voyage which would end at the shipbreaker's yard.

(Portsmouth Evening News)

22 November 1973 and *Albion* is towed to her final resting place, the shipbreaker's yard at Faslane. *(FAAM)*

thousands of wood carvings to choose from on the streets of Mombasa, as well as the ice-cold Tusker lager to enjoy, and on 22 November, duly refreshed, *Albion* sailed and set course for the Gulf of Masirah and the staging post off Oman where, with *Eagle*, *Intrepid* and *Achilles* she would assist in the withdrawal of British forces from the Persian Gulf.

The last act of *Albion's* final deployment east of Suez came on 10 December 1971 when, after embarking four Sea Kings from *Eagle's* 826 Squadron, she was detached at full speed to the Bay of Bengal to render assistance to British citizens caught up in the war between India and Pakistan which resulted, on 17 December, in the Pakistan Army in East Pakistan surrendering and the subsequent establishment of Bangladesh. From the Bay of Bengal *Albion* was ordered to Gan, and on 15 December 40 Commando flew home in time for Christmas.

Albion had to spend Christmas Day in the Indian Ocean, but the New Year was celebrated in style at Cape Town which, for many, was the highlight of the commission. The city produced hospitality on a grand scale with barbecues, receptions, brewery and wine cellar visits, and bus tours. However, it was the private invitations which made everyone feel at home before, on 5 January 1972, *Albion* sailed for the UK. On 20 January 848 Squadron flew off to Culdrose and three days later, on a cold, wet day, *Albion* tied up alongside Pitch House Jetty where many of the families were waiting to welcome the ship.

It was 11 April 1972 before *Albion* sailed from Portsmouth once again and, having embarked 848 Squadron and 42 Commando, she set course for the eastern Mediterranean. Between 20 and 29 April the ship lay off Cyprus landing and supporting the commandos during 'Exercise Double Base'. However, there was time for relaxation and despite the unpredictable weather, leave was granted. In early May the ship took part in 'Exercise Dawn Patrol', a large NATO exercise which involved the interchange of aircraft between the ships, and gave 848 Squadron the opportunity to cross operate their helicopters with those of the USS *Guadalcanal*. During the exercise *Albion* visited Soudhas Bay in Crete and Kavalla in Greece, where she was the first British warship to visit since the end of the Second World War. At the end of the exercise *Albion* left the Mediterranean and, flying the flag of the C-in-C Fleet, Admiral Sir Edward Ashmore KCB CB, she made an official visit to Brest. This involved a brief call at Plymouth to disembark 42 Commando in exchange for a Royal Marine Band, specially for the occasion. On 31 May, having completed her Mediterranean deployment, *Albion* returned to Portsmouth and two days later Captain W. D. M. Staveley RN took command for *Albion's* final six months of operational service.

In mid-June *Albion* steamed north for Rosyth where she received a visit from the Grand Duke of Luxembourg, and she also embarked both 848 Squadron and 45 Commando. She then sailed north again to join the *Fearless* for 'Exercise Strength Trial' off the Orkneys. Later that month she headed south to Rotterdam, via Arbroath, where 45 Commando were landed and 300 Dutch marines, complete with very long hair, were embarked. On 28 June *Albion* made a ceremonial entry into Rotterdam, with both the ship's company and the RNMC lining the flight deck. At the conclusion of the visit *Albion* steamed down the Channel and after disembarking 848 Squadron for Culdrose for the last time, she steamed north to Greenock for Clyde Week.

On 18 July *Albion* was back in Portsmouth and hosting a families' day, when nearly 1,000 relatives joined the ship at Spithead for two hours of displays which gave an opportunity to find out what the 'old man' did when he went to sea. This was followed a few days later by a farewell visit to Dover where choppy seas prevented an open day, but the civic dignitaries were able to say goodbye to the ship which had been adopted by the Confederation of Cinque Ports nearly 19 years before.

Albion returned to Portsmouth for August and on Navy Days the 'old lady' proved as popular as ever with the queues winding their way from Pitch House Jetty to No 2 dry dock which houses HMS *Victory*. In September *Albion* headed for the Norwegian Fjords once again and took part in 'Exercise Strong Express', the largest NATO exercise which had ever been staged. On 10 October she sailed for Canada and visits to St John's, Newfoundland, Halifax NS, Quebec and Montreal. During this deployment she landed 42 Commando at St John, New Brunswick, for Arctic exercises, and Captain Staveley found the water to be so polluted that the ship's evaporators had to be shut down. She also navigated the St Lawrence Seaway which was a tight squeeze in places.

Following the Canadian deployment *Albion* disembarked 42 Commando at Plymouth, flew off 845 Squadron to Culdrose and made her final ceremonial entry into Portsmouth Harbour on Friday 24 November 1972. Hundreds of spectators watched her steam the last few miles along Southsea's seafront, as 16 of 848 Squadron's Wessex helicopters flew overhead in salute and her paying-off pennant streamed aft to the very end of the flight deck. As she came alongside at Middle Slip Jetty there were hundreds of wives, sweethearts and families waiting to greet her, and Captain Staveley rang 'finished with engines' for the last time.

In the week following her arrival the Royal Engineers built an enormous 270ft vehicle bridge to provide access for lorries to drive onto the flight deck in order to remove the heavy gear. This process of decommissioning was an experience which Petty Officer John Stewart remembers vividly: 'It was a sad experience to witness the lingering death of this fine old ship which, during the three years I served in her, had come to be an "old friend" and, although memories fade, I am left with an overwhelming recollection of melancholy of those last few months aboard the ship. Within days of our final return to Portsmouth we were left with only a skeleton ship's company, most of whom were involved in stripping the equipment from various compartments and preparing them for final sealing. This period was not without its mishaps and I recall a fire exercise one evening when we turned on a fire main valve and, instead of water, we got a solid jet of AVCAT. How this happened remains a mystery, but it was fortunate that we did not suffer any real fires.

I was one of five petty officers who kept regular watches on board, carrying out and supervising the safety patrols. As each day passed our patrol area shrank considerably as whole areas of the ship were sealed off. In our HQ a wallboard which showed the ship's deck plans was soon covered with large red chinagraph swathes which indicated the rapid progress of this sealing operation and the rapidly dwindling area which we were still able to patrol. At the same time many of the remaining ship's company received their draft chits and our numbers declined quickly. Personally I remember a feeling of cold desolation pervading the whole ship and, indeed, during the silent hours it was certainly not a place for those of a nervous disposition. I took my final leave of the "old girl" on 25 March 1973, and the next day she was towed out to the reserve fleet moorings in Fareham Creek.'

When *Albion* arrived at the moorings CPO Douglas Norman said his farewells to the ship which, in 1954, he had joined as a Junior Electrician, serving during the first commission, and in which he had served since 1971 as a Chief Electrical Mechanic: 'I will always remember the death knell of the ship when, as the last of the naval personnel to leave the *Albion*, I closed the upper deck screen door for the last time. The poor old *Albion*, which I had known for almost 20 years, was literally just an empty shell. It was very sad and moving for me and as I left her I could not resist one last, lingering look at the rusting grey hulk which had been both my first, and my last, sea-going home.'

Albion lay at her mooring in Fareham Creek for seven months, on the disposal list and waiting for a buyer. In the autumn of 1973 it appeared that she might be saved from the scrapyard, at least for a few years, when a consortium led by Wilson Walker (Engineering) Ltd showed some interest in having the old ship converted to a heavy lift vessel for servicing oil rigs in the fledgling North Sea oil industry. When she was towed from Portsmouth on Monday 22 October 1973 by three ocean-going tugs, *Roysterer*, *Rollicker* and *Typhoon*, it was generally thought that she would undergo conversion on the Clyde for her new role. Unfortunately the plans did not materialize and after lying moored in the River Clyde for three weeks the *Albion* was sold for scrap. She made her final journey, to the breaker's yard at Faslane, on 22 November 1973, 29 years after her first keel plates had been laid at Swan Hunter's shipyard, Newcastle upon Tyne.

Finis

Appendix One

Principal Particulars (As Built)

Length Overall: 737ft

Beam Overall: 128ft

Displacement: 26,118 tons

Draught: 22ft

Armament: 26 radar controlled 40mm Bofors

Aircraft: 35 Sea Hawk/Sea Venom

Main Propulsion Machinery: Twin screw. Two sets Parsons geared turbines. Steam provided by four Admiralty three-drum superheat boilers

SHP: 80,000

Speed: 28 knots

Complement (with embarked squadrons): 1,400

Flight Deck: Interim angled flight deck $5^1/2^°$ giving a 64ft wide landing area. Two aircraft lifts. Two catapults. Six arrester wires

Deck Recognition Letter: Z (1954-1957)
A (1957-1973)

Pennant Number: RO7

Appendix Two

Commanding Officers HMS *Albion*

	Date Appointed:
Captain G.H. Beale DSO OBE RN	2.7.53
Captain W.A.F. Hawkins DSO OBE DSC RN	2.1.55
Captain R.M. Smeeton MBE RN	26.6.56
Captain A.B. Cole DSC RN	10.4.58
Captain F.M.A. Torrens-Spence DSO DSC AFC RN	21.9.59
Captain C.D. Madden MVO DSC RN	10.4.62
Captain J.H. Adams LVO RN	10.5.64
Captain B.C.G. Place VC DSO RN	12.1.66
Captain M.S. Ollivant MBE DSC RN	24.12.67
Captain H.C. Leach RN	3.3.70
Captain J.G. Jungius RN	5.1.71
Captain W. D. M. Staveley RN	2.6.72

Appendix Three

Ship's Badge

Blazon
Barry wavy of two and issuant from the lower a rock all white, thereon a lion sejant affrontee gold, armed and langued red.

Motto:
Fortiter, Fideliter, Feliciter. (Boldly, Faithfully, Successfully).

Designed by Sir Arthur Cochrane 12 June 1947 and approved by Admiral Sir Alexander Madden KCB CBE, Deputy Controller of the Navy & Director of Naval Equipment, on behalf of the Admiralty Board on 21 June 1947.

The name is of geographical origin being the ancient name for the island of Britain. Its Gaelic form is 'Alban' or 'Albany', from the Latin for white, on account of the white chalk cliffs in the Straits of Dover. 'Albion' is still a poetic term for Great Britain.

Badge:
The white rock issuing from waves alludes to our island, and the lion is a symbol of England, as well as being a royal badge. The lion sejant in Heraldry signifies wisdom and counsel.

Heraldic Terms Used:

Barry Wavy:	Undulating barrulets of alternating colours.
Barrulet:	The diminutive of a bar.
Issuant:	Issuing from.
Sejant:	Sitting.
Affrontee:	Facing the observer.
Armed:	In animals and birds: teeth, claws, tusks, talons and beaks. In arrows: the heads – when shown of a different colour to that of their main component.
Langued:	The tongue of a beast or bird.

Appendix Four

HMS *Albion* And The Cinque Ports

HMS *Albion* was adopted by the Confederation of the Cinque Ports at a meeting of Brotherhood and Guestling held at Dover on 24 September 1953, and there was a plaque on the ship's quarterdeck which bore witness to this fact. But what is the history behind this rather complicated sounding statement? What are the Cinque Ports?

The five great ports on the coast of Kent and Sussex - Sandwich, Dover, Hythe, Romney and Hastings - were of considerable importance even before the Norman Conquest in 1066, but it was after the Battle of Hastings that William the Conqueror constituted this whole coastal area into a jurisdiction, separate from the counties in which it lies, under a Warden who exercised jurisdiction - civil, military and naval. Subsequently the 'ancient towns' of Winchelsea and Rye were granted the same privileges as the Cinque (Five) Ports. The chief function of the Cinque Ports in early times was to provide such shipping as was organized for the purpose of state, there being no permanent Navy prior to the reign of Henry VII. For example, during Edward I's reign they were found to produce no fewer than 57 ships, fully equipped and manned at their own cost, though the limit of gratuitous service was 15 days. In return the ports were exempt from taxes and tolls, they had the right to make their own bye-laws, and later had extremely high representation in Parliament. In consequence of the warlike Navy which the Cinque Ports were required to maintain, they became so powerful that they not only undertook piratical expeditions but also waged war and formed confederacies on their own behalf.

However, with the formation of a permanent Navy, the requirements for the Cinque Ports' ships disappeared and gradually by various Acts of Parliament their powers and privileges were removed and their status is now the same as any other municipality. However, the old Courts of Shepway, Brotherhood and Guestling, which used to rule and administer the Cinque Ports, still occasionally meet, but their powers now scarcely extend beyond matters of form. The Lord Warden still presides over the Court of Shepway and appoints JPs within the jurisdiction of the Cinque Ports.

The name 'Albion' was the ancient name of the island of Britain. Its first recorded use was by Aristotle (500 BC) in a treatise on the world. Its derivation is probably Gaelic and it was the original name of Britain among the Celtic population.

Appendix Five

Former *Albions*

The First *Albion* 1763-1794.

A 74-gun ship of 1,662 tons, launched at Deptford on 16 May 1763. She was commissioned in 1770 at Chatham and in June 1773 was present at the first Royal Review of the Fleet by HM King George III at Spithead. On 6 July 1779 *Albion* was one of the 21 ships of the line under Vice-Admiral Sir John Byron, which engaged a French fleet of 25 sail of the line under Admiral D' Eastaing off Grenada in the West Indies. The action, in which the British lost 183 killed and 346 wounded, was indecisive. In December of the same year, *Albion* took part in an attack on a French convoy of 26 ships off St Lucia. Nine French vessels were captured and four driven ashore. In 1780 *Albion* took part in Rodney's three actions with the French under Rear-Admiral de Guichen off Martinique. In the second, *Albion* led the van and received more of the enemy's fire than any other British ship in this famous action. In 1794 she was converted to a coastal defence ship, but was unfortunately wrecked in the River Swin, the crew being saved by the frigate *Astraea*.

The Second *Albion* 1798-1803.

An armed sloop of 366 tons, built at Deptford in 1798. She mounted 20 guns and was based on Sheerness, being sold out of service in 1803.

The Third *Albion* 1803-1836.

A 74-gun ship of the line of 1,740 tons. She was launched on the Thames in 1802, and in May 1803 began a long and eventful career by capturing the French 40-gun frigate *Franchise* in the Channel. *Albion* was at this time part of Admiral the Hon William Cornwallis' fleet which was engaged in the blockade of Brest. In 1806 *Albion*, assisted by HMS *Sceptre*, captured the heavily armed French privateer *La Clarisse* in the East Indies. In May 1814 the flag of Rear-Admiral Cockburn was hoisted in HMS *Albion*, and the ship subsequently took part in many actions of the American War of 1812-1815. Her boats carried out attacks on shipping in Chesapeake Bay and in June she assisted in the blockade of an American squadron in the Patuxent River. In July she proceeded up the Potomac, landed her detachment of Royal Marines and captured Leonardstown, destroying a large quantity of the enemy's stores. In the following month *Albion's* boats assisted in the destruction of the American squadron in the Patuxent River, and in January 1815 she reduced the fort at Point Peter with her guns, recapturing the British Indiaman *Harcourt* and taking Cumberland Island by storm. On 27 August 1816 *Albion* was part of the Mediterranean Fleet under Lord Exmouth which bombarded Algiers. The ship fired 4,110 rounds of shot in the course of the action and sustained the loss of three killed and 15 wounded. The *Albion* was again in a hot action at the Battle of Navarino on 20 October 1827, when her second-in-command, Commander John Campbell RN, was killed, together with eight others and 50 wounded. The ship was broken up at Deptford in 1836.

The Fourth *Albion* 1842-1884.

This *Albion* was a 90-gun ship of the line of 3,110 tons, launched at Devonport in 1842. During the 1840s she formed part of the Mediterranean Fleet and there is a story that her First Lieutenant coated the ship with gold leaf and silver paint, thus earning her the nickname, 'The Gilded Toy Shop'. On 21 June 1854, on the eve of her departure for the Crimea, HM Queen Victoria visited the *Albion* at Spithead. Her commanding officer, Captain Stephen Lushington RN (later Admiral Sir Stephen Lushington), commanded the Naval Brigade, which was landed to assist the army before Sebastopol. The ship was badly damaged by fire whilst bombarding this fortress. In 1861 *Albion* was fitted with a propeller and a steam engine of 1,835 hp. In 1884 she was sold for breaking up.

The Fifth *Albion* 1901-1919.

The fifth *Albion* was a twin-screw first-class armoured Canopus class battleship of 12,950 tons, armed with four 12-inch breech-loading guns. She was launched at Blackwall on 21 June 1898 by the Duchess of York (later HM Queen Mary), and the ship was commissioned in 1901. *Albion* joined the China Station where she remained until 1905, when she joined the Channel Fleet. In April 1906 she was in Commissioned Reserve at Chatham, undergoing an engine and boiler refit which lasted until December that year. She joined the Home Fleet in February 1907 and a month later she joined the Atlantic Fleet. In August 1909 she became Parent Ship of the 4th Division, Home Fleet at the Nore. In August 1914 she joined the 8th Battle Squadron, Channel Fleet and she was then sent to the Cape of Good Hope and East Africa until February 1915 when she was sent to the Dardanelles. During the bombardment of the Turkish defences on 28 April and 2 May 1915 she was damaged by enemy shellfire and temporarily grounded off Gaba Tepe. In October 1915 she transported troops to Salonika and then, in April 1916, she returned home, where she was stationed on the east coast as a guardship. In 1918 she was sent to Devonport where she was used as an accommodation ship and in December 1919 she was sold to T. W. Ward of Morecambe, Lancashire, for breaking up. She arrived in Morecambe on 6 January 1920 and her demolition was finally completed in November 1921.

Acknowledgements:

My thanks to Admiral of the Fleet Sir William Staveley GCB DL, the *Albion's* last Commanding Officer, for his help and for kindly writing the foreword to this book. My thanks also to *Albion's* other Commanding Officers as follows:-

Rear-Admiral John Adams CB LVO.

Vice-Admiral Sir James Jungius KBE.

Admiral of the Fleet Sir Henry Leach GCB DL.

Rear-Admiral Colin Madden CB CBE DSC.

Captain Martin Ollivant MBE DSC RN.

The late Rear-Admiral Godfrey Place VC CB CVO DSC.

Captain Michael Torrens-Spence DSO DSC AFC RN.

I must also thank the following for both their memories of the *Albion* and for the loan of photographs:-

Mr Michael Axford: Mr Raymond Blaber: Mr Denis Burgess: Dr Ian L. Buxton, Reader in Marine Transport, University of Newcastle: Mr Michael Cassar, Valletta, Malta: Mr Gordon Chiverton: Mr Neville Clements: Mr Sydney Elmes: Mr N.G. Frost: Admiral Sir Anthony Griffin GCB: Mr Peter Harris: Mr Terence Higgins: Brenda Jacob, Librarian, *The News*, Hilsea, Portsmouth: Mr R.G. Jelley: Mr J. Livermore: Mr Douglas K. Norman: Mr N.E.D. Parkinson, RO8 HMS *Bulwark* Association: Mr John Stewart: Vice-Admiral Sir Patrick Symons KBE: Mr A. Trotman, Royal Naval Museum, Portsmouth: Mr Michael Turner, New Zealand: Mr A. Vicary: Mr William Walker: Mr Donald Whyte: Mr Robin V. Williams: Mr R. Wilson: Mr Peter Wood: Finally thanks also to my wife Freda and to my two daughters, Caroline and Louise.

Special thanks must go to:-

Mr David Richardson, Research Officer, Fleet Air Arm Museum, RNAS Yeovilton, for providing numerous photographs from the Museum's collection. Readers wishing to purchase copies of these photographs should contact, or visit, the Fleet Air Arm Museum, RNAS Yeovilton, Nr Ilchester, Somerset BA22 8HT. All the photographs which are available from the Museum are marked (FAAM).

Mr Brian Conroy, New Zealand maritime artist for his magnificent water-colour painting of the *Albion* during her 1958/1959 world cruise. Mr Conroy is happy to undertake commission work for readers who can contact him by writing to PO Box 50-426, Porirua, New Zealand.

Mr Ian Spashett of FotoFlite for allowing me to use his company's magnificent shots of the *Albion* during her farewell visit to Dover on 25 July 1972. Readers wishing to purchase copies of these photographs should contact FotoFlite, Littlestone Road, New Romney, Kent TN28 8LN.

Rear-Admiral John Adams, Lt-Cdr Bernard Lyons, Captain Martin Ollivant and Commander Ian Hamilton for lending me their photographs, albums, diaries and colour transparencies.